Social Freedom
The Path to Wellbeing

Social Freedom: The Path to Wellbeing
© Deborah Devaal 2024

All rights reserved. No part of this publication may be reproduced, stored in a retrieval system, or transmitted in any form or by any means, electronic, mechanical, photocopying, recording or otherwise, without the prior written permission of the author.

Deborah Devaal is recognised as the creator of this content and has asserted her right to be identified as the author of this work.

This publication is designed to provide accurate and authoritative information in regard to the subject matter covered. It is sold with the understanding that neither the author nor the publisher is engaged in rendering legal, investment, accounting or other professional services. While the publisher and author have used their best efforts in preparing this book, they make no representations or warranties with respect to the accuracy or completeness of the contents of this book and specifically disclaim any implied warranties of merchantability or fitness for a particular purpose. No warranty may be created or extended by sales representatives or written sales materials. The advice and strategies contained herein may not be suitable for your situation. You should consult with a professional when appropriate. Neither the publisher nor the author shall be liable for any loss of profit or any other commercial damages, including but not limited to special, incidental, consequential, per-sonal, or other damages.

ISBN: 978-0-646-88549-0 (Paperback)

 A catalogue record for this book is available from the National Library of Australia

Illustrations: Jett Fahey
Cover Design: Deborah Devaal and Jett Fahey
Format and Typeset: Deborah Devaal and Clark & Mackay
Published by Deborah Devaal and Clark & Mackay

Proudly printed in Australia by Clark & Mackay

Contents

Preface 7
Introduction 11

Social Freedom and Wellbeing 13
A Rainbow of Emotions 17
SFUC–Is It a Swear Word? 19
Understanding the Seven Emotions 23
Breakdown or Breakthrough? 39
The Wellbeing Cup 43
The Seven Stages 45
The Awareness Stage 51
The Acceptance Stage 71
The Accountability Stage 87

The Empowerment Stage 111

The Action Stage 139

The Achievement Stage 155

The Contribution Stage 173

The Journey Back Home 193

What's Next 195

Home Is Where the Heart Is 201

A Picture Speaks a Thousand Words 203

Seeking Help 205

Acknowledgements 207

About the Author 209

To everyone who would like to improve their wellbeing

Preface

In a world where societal expectations and norms often shape our actions and decisions, the concept of social freedom becomes a beacon of empowerment and self-discovery. This book explores the intricate relationship between social freedom, our emotions and overall wellbeing, shedding light on how we can harness autonomy to improve mental health and find fulfilment. Recognising that true freedom lies in understanding our emotions, it can serve as a transformative tool on our path to wellbeing.

In my roles as an Art Therapist and Wellbeing Coach, I have worked with a wide variety of clients who were striving to improve their wellbeing. From young clients experiencing mental health challenges, to entrepreneurs experiencing burnout, to parents overwhelmed by juggling the many aspects of daily life.

Over time, I have crafted a method to assist them all in reaching the state of wellbeing they were looking for. In our weekly sessions, I found myself sketching images, and jotting down tools and practices, for them to take home. After repeating this process numerous times, I realised it would be so much more convenient to have them all in one place, and the idea for this book was born. I hope it will help you find your own social freedom as you discover your path to wellbeing.

—Deborah Devaal

This book is dedicated to my beautiful children. You are my biggest inspiration. May you always create yourself a life of fulfilment and share your abundance of love.

Introduction

Welcome to *Social Freedom: The Path to Wellbeing*. This book aims to help you feel empowered to reach your maximum potential and live your best life. You don't have to feel helpless, confused, or stressed. Instead, you have the power to take control of your wellbeing journey and create a life of fulfilment. Let me help you unleash the best version of yourself.

Armed with the right tools and a deeper understanding of our emotions, we can improve our ability to heal and thrive in the world around us, thereby improving our overall wellbeing. When we experience feelings of anxiety, sadness or overwhelm, we can learn to regulate these emotions with the appropriate tools, leading to a heightened sense of presence, contentment and balance. No longer do we need to feel like we are just surviving, emotionally affected by our external environment, past experiences and old beliefs. Instead, we can become the creators of our lives, taking charge and assuming full responsibility for our path. Now, that is what I call freedom! And believe me, we are fully capable of creating this reality for ourselves.

I will show you how, step by step, as we work our way through this book together, which is divided into three sections:

Part 1, Social Freedom, invites you to explore how understanding your emotions can serve as a fundamental tool in creating a more balanced life. I encourage you to take your time exploring this section, as it provides insights into using emotional identification as a roadmap to achieve greater stability.

In Part 2, The Path to Wellbeing, we focus on improving your wellbeing through the lens of the seven stages of the Wellbeing Cup and its transformative potential. Here, you'll find easy-to-use tools, exercises, valuable insights and strategies for personal growth.

Part 3, The Journey Back Home, explores the deeper connection to your true self and how to incorporate all the knowledge and insights you've gained into your everyday existence.

I invite you to join me on this journey with an open mind and a willingness to explore the depths of your being. Together, we'll unlock the secrets to a balanced and fulfilling life. Remember, you are not alone on this path, and I am here to support you every step of the way. Let's begin.

While the cases presented in this book are based on real people, I've taken care to alter names and significant details to protect their privacy and identities.

Social Freedom and Wellbeing

You might be wondering why this book is called *Social Freedom* and what does it have to do with welbeing. Through my work as an Art Therapist and Wellbeing Coach, I've had the privilege to work with people of all ages, from children to adults, who, despite their unique life challenges, all had something in common. They shared a desire for a deeper understanding and control over their emotions, often feeling unequipped with the necessary tools. They also felt like they often didn't fit in with others, like they were misunderstood and alone. Stuck in this cycle, they were seeking ways to improve their lives, searching for a sense of freedom and inner contentment.

Let's start by talking about social freedom. In this book, we use it to describe a state of mind where you feel like you can be yourself. When you have social freedom, you can say what you think, connect with others and handle social situations easily. It also means you can set boundaries, express what you need and deal with social problems better. In simple terms, social freedom is about being yourself and feeling good about it.

Now, onto wellbeing. Wellbeing is about feeling happy, healthy and balanced in different parts of your life, like your feelings, body, friends and even your soul. It involves having a purpose, good relationships and being able to handle tough times. Basically, it's about having a good life overall.

One big step to attaining both social freedom and wellbeing is understanding and managing your emotions. Throughout this book, we'll explore the role of emotions and how they can make our lives better.

Part 1
Social Freedom

A Rainbow of Emotions

Emotions are reflections of our innermost being; they are the vibrant colours that paint the canvas of our consciousness, shaping our thoughts, actions and interactions with the world around us. They're sometimes hard to grasp, a bit tricky to put into words, yet powerful enough to knock us off balance.

It is not always easy to deal with our emotions, as they can be very complex and challenging to navigate. They can reveal the depths of our desires, fears and aspirations. When we find ourselves on an emotional rollercoaster, seeking comfort in creative expressions such as music, movies or art can often help us make sense of what's going on inside. It is like the artists have taken those complex feelings and turned them into something we can instantly relate to. We don't need to overthink it; we just feel understood and get a release.

For instance, think about that song you play on repeat when you need a confidence boost or that TV series you binge-watch when your heart is heavy with sadness. These creative outlets speak to our souls, offering a sense of understanding and release. Similarly, art has a unique ability to mirror our emotions, making us feel deeply connected.

But here's the thing: just as these creative mediums can connect with us, we also have the power to connect with our own emotions without getting overwhelmed. Sure, emotions can be intense, but by dedicating time to understand and navigate our emotions with a simple framework, we can get a better grip on them, understand them and even let them guide us.

Let's explore how we can effectively do this.

SFUC Is It A Swear Word?

Emotions serve as our personal alert system, nudging us to take action. However, we're not meant to get stuck in them forever. Equipping ourselves with the right tools to deal with our differing emotions opens a world of freedom, allowing us to progress, reconnect with ourselves and grow personally.

Now, about SFUC, it might sound a bit like a swear word, but don't fear, it's not! (Well, unless you want it to be, but that's entirely up to you) It's actually an acronym for something pretty interesting and is a handy tool to have on hand. We can apply this acronym to understand our emotions better.

Stop
Feel
Understand
Connect

Let's imagine for example that you're engulfed in a wave of anger, feeling the urge to lash out or explode; it can be like riding a rollercoaster with no brakes, an intense whirlwind of emotions threatening to overwhelm you. Emotions can really take us for a wild ride if we're not careful. There is so much going on at that moment, but what if you quietly whispered "SFUC" to yourself at that moment and applied the following steps?

1. STOP: Take a deep breath (and when I say 'deep', I mean take a really good and deep breath that fills your belly, making it expand).

2. FEEL: Check in with yourself; how do you feel?

Can you describe to yourself how you feel in this moment? For example, I can feel my heart racing, I feel hot, and I feel like yelling and punching. I feel angry.

3. UNDERSTAND: Recognise that emotions are temporary experiences. They're simply signals from your body and mind, indicating that something is happening internally. Instead of being overwhelmed by them, understand that they're like messengers saying, "Hey, pay attention to this!"

Trying to push an emotion away is not the best idea; it might work for a while, but it's bound to pop back up eventually, and as mentioned before, an emotion is designed to alert us to something. So, examining those emotions deeply is the way to go. For example, why do I feel so angry? Asking why you feel angry is like digging for clues. What triggered you? Was it a specific event or situation? But don't stop there – because sometimes, there might be deeper layers to uncover. Are there underlying factors or past experiences that contributed to this anger? By examining emotions deeply, we uncover valuable insights.

4. CONNECT: Now that you have a better understanding of the emotion, you can use the tools and exercises provided in this book to reconnect with yourself, work with the emotion and pursue personal growth which is something we will explore in greater depth in upcoming chapters.

By applying these steps, you can change the way you think, feel and act, taking charge of your emotions. Before we do this, let's look at some common emotions that can take us on a rollercoaster.

UNDERSTANDING THE SEVEN EMOTIONS

Each of these seven emotions carries its own distinct message. I'm highlighting them because they often play a central role in mental health challenges within my professional practice.

Gaining clarity on a specific emotion is a great starting point. When my clients can pinpoint what they're feeling, it becomes much simpler to figure out the best way to address it. It's like having a map to navigate through the emotional terrain and find the most effective path forward.

In this section, we'll dive deep into these emotions and how we can explore them. We'll take a closer look at each emotion, using the SFUC method as a guide to break them down one by one. Building upon this foundation, Part 2 of the book will introduce a range of easy-to-use wellbeing tools and practices to further develop emotional regulation and overall wellbeing.

Note: If these feelings persist or interfere with your daily life, it may be helpful to seek support from a mental health professional or healthcare provider.

anxious | worried, nervous |

I am feeling worried or nervous, I am having anxious thoughts about future events.

Stop: Take a deep breath

Feel: Ask yourself, "how am I feeling?"

Example: I am feeling restless, my heart is racing, I am breathing fast, I am feeling anxious.

Understand: Why am I feeling like this?

I am experiencing anxiety because my thoughts are about future events or scenarios. These haven't happened yet, and I am most likely imagining a worst-case scenario.

Connect: Try answering the following questions:

1. How can I bring myself back to the present moment?
2. Is my current thought accurate?
3. How can I feel more grounded in this moment?

sad | flat, empty |

I have information to process that does not align with how I want things to be. As I work to accept this, I grieve for what I have lost or am losing.

Stop: Take a deep breath

Feel: Take a moment to ask yourself, "How am I feeling?"

Example: I am feeling flat and empty. I feel like crying. I am feeling sad.

Understand: Why am I feeling like this?

I'm dealing with information that doesn't match my desired outcome. While I'm trying to come to terms with it, I'm also feeling a sense of loss, and this is making me sad.

Connect: Try answering the following questions:

1. Is it possible for me to embrace my current situation and accept the feelings that arise?
2. Is it possible for me to practice self-compassion for the loss I am experiencing?
3. Are there little moments of joy I can discover every day?
4. What is it that matters most to me that I can connect with to boost my positivity and sense of fulfilment?
5. Have I established a self-care routine that I can rely on when I feel like this?

upset | resentful, angry |

I feel upset because something unpleasant has happened, or I may sense that I or someone I care about is not quite understood, is not receiving the respect they deserve or is being treated unfairly in some way.

Stop: Take a deep breath.

Feel: Take a moment to ask yourself, "How am I feeling?"

Example: I am so upset this happened. I feel like I am going to burst, I am so angry. My heart is beating fast, and I feel like yelling loudly.

Understand: Why am I feeling like this?

I'm experiencing anger because I believe something didn't unfold as it should have, or someone's behaviour seemed inappropriate from my perspective. This left me feeling as if I or someone I care about wasn't treated respectfully or fairly.

Connect: Try answering the following questions:

1. Is what I am feeling based on solid evidence, or am I making assumptions? What are the concrete facts?
2. Can I take a step back and view this from a wider perspective? Am I feeling distressed about the current situation, or does this somehow trigger memories of past experiences?

Social Freedom

3. Is it necessary for me to establish stronger boundaries in this situation?
4. What steps can I take to improve communication in this situation?
5. Am I becoming entangled in matters that aren't my responsibility? How can I narrow my focus to what truly concerns me? How can I take responsibility for my role, redirect my energy and initiate positive changes if possible?

insecure | unsure, constraint |

I have feelings of not being good enough or worthy, and this is impacting how I handle situations and people in my life.

Stop: Take a deep breath

Feel: Take a moment to ask yourself, "How am I feeling?"

Example: I am unsure about the situation, so I don't feel comfortable saying anything as I don't want to look odd. Everyone is probably looking at me, which is making me feel nervous.

Understand: Why am I feeling like this?

Feelings of insecurity and unworthiness can significantly impact how I handle situations and interact with people in my life. These feelings often lead to self-doubt and a lack of self-confidence. This can make it challenging to express myself authentically and make decisions confidently. These feelings can create a self-fulfilling cycle where I perceive myself as inadequate, which then influences how I engage with others and the world around me.

Connect: Try answering the following questions:

1. What could be the root cause of these feelings I have about being unworthy or not good enough?
2. Am I conscious of the fact that I am a unique individual with my own strengths and values?

Social Freedom

3. Am I using my unique strengths to propel myself forward in life?
4. Do I have a clear understanding of my values, and am I fully committed to standing behind them without any doubt?
5. Am I actively seeking opportunities to act on matters that align with my values?
6. Am I playing small and limiting my potential? What is driving this behaviour?

overwhelmed | confused, paralysed |

I experience feeling mentally or emotionally flooded, where the weight of tasks, responsibilities and stimuli becomes almost suffocating, making it difficult for me to cope effectively.

Stop: Take a deep breath.

Feel: Take a moment to ask yourself, "How am I feeling?"

Example: It feels like everything is happening all at once, it's becoming quite overwhelming, and I'm recognising the need to take a step back.

Understand: Why am I feeling like this?

I'm experiencing feelings of overwhelm because life is moving at a pace that's challenging for my mind and nervous system to keep up with. This feeling can arise when there's a mismatch between the demands placed on me and my perceived ability to handle those demands. As a result, I may feel paralysed and find it difficult to take action.

Connect: Try answering the following questions:

1. Can I think of strategies I can use to slow things down, to bring a sense of calm into my life?
2. What is most important right now?

3. How can I channel my energy and time into the most important tasks and objectives?
4. Can I think of a way to deconstruct complex issues into smaller, manageable parts?
5. How can I develop a step-by-step plan to move forward on these smaller parts, thereby creating a sense of accomplishment and also soothing my nervous system?

drained | depleted, exhausted |

I feel emotionally worn out due to accumulated stress.

Stop: Take a deep breath.

Feel: Take a moment to ask yourself, "How am I feeling?"

Example: I don't have the energy to participate. Everything seems too hard, and I don't know what to do. I have lost or am losing the ability to feel excited about my current life situation. I feel depleted and am in a state of imbalance, feeling empty and exhausted.

Understand: Why am I feeling like this?

My mind, body and soul are yearning for a recharge, but I have nothing left to give. As my reserves are getting lower, I feel the need to replenish. An ongoing and accumulating stressor slowly is or was sapping away my energy reserves. It's like a constant drain on my mental and emotional resources.

Connect: Try answering the following questions:

1. What creates energy for me, and what takes it away?
2. In which areas of my life am I neglecting myself?
3. In what areas of my life am I not fully embracing my potential?

4. What activities or experiences bring me a sense of joy and fulfilment?
5. What are my true emotions and thoughts regarding this specific situation in my life that's causing me to feel drained?

hopeless | despair, helplessness |

I feel like I have lost, or have almost lost, all hope for things to turn out well. I feel that a positive outcome is out of reach and that there is no way to improve or change the situation for the better.

Stop: Take a deep breath.

Feel: Take a moment to ask yourself, "How am I feeling?"

Example: I feel like there is no light at the end of the tunnel, I don't know what to do.

Understand: Why am I feeling like this?

I feel like this because I feel trapped in this situation. I can't see a way out or see how it can improve, therefore I feel like giving up.

Connect: Try answering the following questions:

1. How can I take steps to make progress and improve my situation?
2. What does it require for me to feel supported?
3. Where do I have meaningful connections with others, and where can I find my supportive community?
4. How can I keep developing those connections further with my community?

5. Is it possible to create a plan and to take the steps required to create those connections?
6. What areas of my life represent opportunities for growth?

Exploring each emotion individually is very helpful, yet, while riding the rollercoaster of our emotions, it's not uncommon to feel like all sorts of feelings are starting to crash in at once. It can feel like a bunch of emotions are doing a crazy dance inside us, making it difficult to identify each emotion individually. This can feel extremely overwhelming and here's the thing – if we don't let these feelings out, they can pile up and make us feel like we're drowning in them.

This intense feeling can lead to a loss of clarity about our surroundings and make us feel disconnected from the people around us. We might pull away just when we could use some support, or do something impulsive to ease the pressure, projecting our feelings of being overwhelmed on them. Ever noticed how blaming others or lashing out, even if just for a moment, can make things feel a bit lighter? Only for the pressure to return shortly after.

In the face of intense emotions, we sometimes don't want to deal with the uneasiness of feelings. We often look for a quick fix, numbing ourselves with busyness, substances or distractions to temporarily escape discomfort. We think that a quick and comforting fix helps us forget about those

Social Freedom

overwhelming feelings for a bit, and by pushing them down, we can feel like we are giving ourselves some breathing space.

But here's the real deal: for lasting relief, we must invest time in untangling, understanding and working with these emotions. Only then can we fully show up in the world, staying present and true to ourselves. We can do this by using practical tools and wellbeing practices that help us gain clarity and provide a framework that helps us understand and regulate our emotions.

How do we achieve this balanced state? In Part 2, we delve deeper into this process by exploring the transformative seven stages of the Wellbeing Cup.

Breakdown or Breakthrough?

It's up to us to take charge of our emotional wellbeing and make the needed changes. When we experience painful emotions, as we learned through the SFUC method, they can be opportunities for learning and personal growth, a way to help find balance in our lives. What if we saw these uncomfortable feelings as a chance to discover what's on the other side? Feelings like, you're heading for a breakdown, could now turn into a breakthrough – how amazing is that?

Now that we have a better understanding of some of the messages our emotions carry, let's talk about what balance really means. Balance in emotional wellbeing represents a state where our emotions are neither overwhelming nor suppressed. It means, having the ability to acknowledge and express our feelings in a healthy way, without letting them control us. It involves understanding the ebb and flow of emotions, recognising their messages and responding to them with resilience and self-awareness. Emotional balance doesn't mean feeling happy all the time; rather, it implies being in tune with our emotions. It's about maintaining mental stability to be able to navigate our way through life.

How can we keep our minds stable and calm? How do we move from feeling anxious to feeling present or from feeling overwhelmed to feeling in control? There isn't a quick fix for this, but we can use tools and practices to help us find that balance. By incorporating these practices, we can improve our overall wellbeing and mental health. They're things we do every day to make ourselves feel better. Little by little, we get closer to feeling balanced and free from the emotional ups and downs that we used to experience.

Here are the balanced feelings associated with our seven emotions, as discussed in this chapter. Achieving this sense of balance is not as impossible as it might seem right now. In the next part of this book, I'll demonstrate how you can do it. We'll look at wellbeing practices using the Wellbeing Cup and also look at your emotions to unlock your full potential.

Hopeless → Fulfilled
Drained → Energised
Overwhelmed → In Control
Insecure → Worthy
Upset → Balanced
Sad → Content
Anxious → Present

Part 2
The Path to Wellbeing

The Wellbeing Cup

Living a life of wellbeing is about having a sense of contentment and harmony in all areas of our lives, including our feelings, body, friends and even our soul. It involves having a sense of purpose, meaningful relationships and having the resilience to navigate life's challenges. Ultimately, it's about experiencing overall satisfaction and fulfilment.

When we develop a sound understanding of our wellbeing, we unlock the key to understanding ourselves on a deeper level. Armed with this knowledge, we can fully embrace life and actualise the dreams we've long held in our hearts. Within the journey of the path to wellbeing, lies the roadmap towards creating this deeper connection with our inner selves, paving the way for positive changes. Through consistent engagement in wellbeing practices, each of us have the opportunity to cultivate and strengthen this connection that serves as the foundation for a fulfilling life.

Imagine your personal wellbeing as a cup. It is at its fullest when brimming with feelings of presence, contentment, balance, worthiness, control, energy and fulfilment. On the flip side, when you feel anxious, sad, upset, insecure, overwhelmed, drained or hopeless, it's like slowly emptying your cup until there's almost nothing left, leaving you feeling depleted and disconnected.

Experiencing a sense of disconnection or detachment often indicates that we're not completely in alignment with our true selves. To shake off this numbness, we must ground ourselves in practices that awaken our senses and make room for personal growth. Navigating the path to wellbeing involves a delicate balance of releasing what no longer serves us and being open to new experiences. It's a journey that requires commitment and patience, as we take it step by step and do not look for shortcuts, understanding that meaningful change doesn't have to happen overnight.

The Seven Stages

Letting go of what's familiar, even if it causes pain and suffering, isn't always easy. Our mind can easily trick us into believing that the painful facts we are confronted with, do not exist or are not really that important after all. This psychological defence-mechanism is known as denial. Denial often shows up as feeling restless, stuck or bored as we try to avoid the hard work required for change.

However, once we move past denial, we enter the stage of awareness. This is when we become conscious of our role in our healing journey. Often triggered by a crisis, illness or moment of awakening, awareness serves as a wake-up call, shedding light on why we find ourselves in our current situation. Strong emotions may accompany this stage as if a spotlight is suddenly shining on issues we've subconsciously tried to ignore.

As the issue or the life situation breaks through the barrier of denial, we must approach it with deep compassion for ourselves. It's time to take an honest and clear look at what we're facing. Our thoughts, sensations and emotions serve as forms of communication between our body and mind. When we experience them, it's a signal that something is trying to emerge and raise our awareness.

Now, let's turn our attention to our Wellbeing Cup for guidance, using the seven stages as a compass for understanding. We're on a journey through these stages, uncovering where and how we can channel our efforts to achieve optimal results.

Allow me to guide you through the seven stages that make up your Wellbeing Cup. We'll start from the bottom and work our way up, gradually filling your cup to the brim.

For example, when anxiety arises about a certain situation, we feel uncomfortable, our hearts may race, and we worry. Something is attempting to communicate with us here (Awareness stage). We acknowledge our current feelings with self-compassion, understanding that whatever arises is precisely what we need to see, feel, hear or experience to move forward to the next phase. We let go of resistance to push away discomfort and instead lean into it (*Acceptance stage*). We connect with this moment and ourselves.

Now is not the time for distractions, numbing or avoidance. We open up to the raw vulnerability of this moment and take full accountability for ourselves and how we cope with the situation (*Accountability stage*). Our body and mind need us to take charge, seek opportunities for healing and regulating ourselves.

What can we do at this moment? What are our options? This is the point where we access our wellbeing tools. With the right tools and the belief that we can change our situation, we can turn discomfort or pain into an opportunity for growth (*Empowerment stage*).

Now, we are ready to take action and apply the tools to make necessary changes (*Action stage*). As we take action and feel a sense of forward movement, we gain a feeling of achievement (*Achievement stage*). This gives us the energy and confidence to continue creating opportunities to connect with our authentic selves, the people we love and our community. We have reached a stage in our wellbeing where our cup is overflowing, and we have so much to give. We are now in a position to contribute from a place of love in our own unique way (*Contribution stage*).

Our goal is to fill our cup to the brim until it overflows, leading to a state of 'ful-filment'. However, not only can we progress through the different stages to attain fulfilment, but we can also use each stage individually to rebalance our emotions. When we find ourselves experiencing a specific emotion, we can select the corresponding wellbeing stage to help regulate that emotion. Building upon the understanding we've gained through the SFUC method, the Wellbeing Cup becomes a tool for reconnecting with ourselves, shedding what no longer serves us and creating opportunities for personal growth. This is where the simultaneous process of receiving and letting go takes place.

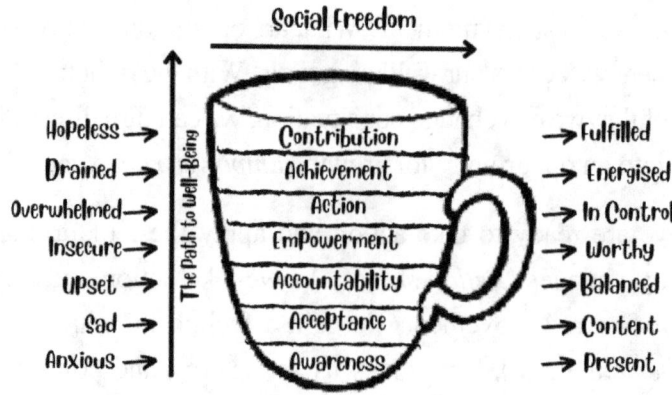

As you can see in the image above, the path towards wellbeing takes us through various stages within the Wellbeing Cup, ultimately reaching a state of fulfilment. Simultaneously, the road to social freedom involves understanding and balancing our emotions. When these elements are combined, they pave the way to a deeper connection to ourselves, a sound mental state and an overall sense of wellbeing.

In the upcoming chapters, we will explore each stage of the Wellbeing Cup, the tools we can use for navigating these stages and how we can regulate our emotions at the same time. Armed with this insight, we will start to feel a shift; now, we are the creators of our lives, taking charge and taking full responsibility for our path. It will be transformative as you notice yourself being less emotionally influenced by your external environment, your past and old beliefs, while simultaneously experiencing a strong sense of empowerment.

So, let's first delve into the foundational principles, the Awareness and Acceptance stages. In these initial phases, we lay the groundwork for meaningful progress, setting the stage for the momentum we'll build in the Accountability Stage and onwards.

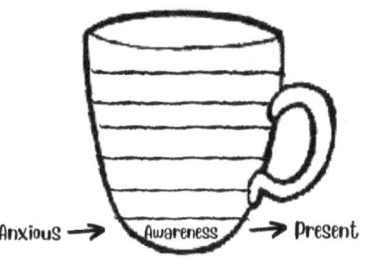

The Awareness Stage

The Awareness stage is the first stage in the Wellbeing Cup and marks an important moment in our journey. If you picked up this book, you're likely seeking change or growth in your life. Perhaps a significant event or realisation has prompted this exploration. Welcome to the Awareness stage.

This stage is often triggered by a crisis, illness or a profound awakening. Awareness means the quality or state of 'being' aware and understanding that something is happening or exists. The awareness stage can therefore feel like a wake-up call, where we start to understand why we've found ourselves in our current situation. This stage can be accompanied by intense emotions, feeling like a sudden spotlight is shining on an issue we may have been unconsciously avoiding.

Remember, as we discussed previously, when an issue or life situation breaks through the barrier of resistance or denial, our body and mind are trying to communicate with us through our thoughts, sensations, and emotions. They are signalling to us, trying to capture our attention and urging us to take a clear and honest look at what we are facing, making us aware.

The awareness stage highlights the importance of staying present, connecting with reality and grounding ourselves in the moment. It encourages us to release resistance and denial and to fully embrace whatever arises, even if it feels challenging. During this phase, we also shed the weight of negative inner chatter, recognising that it consumes valuable energy that could be better directed towards progress, personal growth and nurturing self-esteem. Anxiety may sneak in during this stage, fuelled by worries about the past or the future. It serves as a reminder of the work ahead, which itself can provoke anxiety. Yet, it's precisely during these moments that we must extend self-compassion and understand that whatever emerges is an important part of our journey towards growth. So, what tools can support us as we navigate this stage, particularly when anxiety or life's unexpected challenges, such as illnesses or crises, arise?

Mastering the Inner Voice

Let's talk about that inner voice we all have – you know the one I'm referring to, right? It's the negative one – those repetitive thoughts that just won't quit. They linger and take control of our minds, breeding anxiety and making us feel downright miserable.

We're all familiar with them, and we understand that most of the time, they're not doing us any favours. These thoughts often stem from various sources like past beliefs, trauma, societal expectations or the influence of social media, among others. They're shaped by our personal history, casting a shadow over our judgement and distorting our perception of reality. That's precisely why it's important to recognise that when anxiety is linked to a thought, we should dive deeper into it.

It's completely normal to have this negative inner chatter. Sometimes, it's passed down through generations or is ingrained by what we absorb from media, both of which can impact our thought patterns. The key here is to understand that these are just thoughts and that they aren't necessarily accurate reflections of reality. Two people can have entirely different thoughts about the same situation – one might perceive it positively, while the other might lean towards negativity. The difference arises from their individual conditioning and beliefs. That's why it's beneficial to pause and ask ourselves, "Is this thought suitable for this situation? Is it accurate? And how can I bring more clarity to examine it?"

The Inner Voice Exercise

As we engage in the Inner Voice Exercise, we're basically redefining our relationship with our thoughts. It's like putting on a new pair of glasses, free from the influence of past beliefs, allowing us to see things with greater clarity.

Below, you'll find some examples of thoughts that can overwhelm and dominate our minds, along with instructions on how to apply the Inner Voice Exercise to tackle the inner chatter effectively.

- Step 1: List the troublesome thought in the first column.
- Step 2: Question the truth of this thought and write down the actual reality in the second column.
- Step 3: Reflect on how this reality feels for you. Can you release the old thoughts and embrace this new reality? Record your response in the third column.
- Step 4: Explore the possibility of transforming the old thought into a positive one. Note your answer in the fourth column.

Now, we are observing our new thought through a different lens, one free from past beliefs and conditioning, offering us greater clarity. You can even transform this new thought into an affirmation. Consider jotting it down on a sticky note and placing it somewhere visible, ready for those moments when negative inner chatter re-emerges.

1 THE THOUGHT	2 THE REALITY	3 CAN I LEAVE THIS THOUGHT BEHIND	4 CAN I RESHAPE THIS THOUGHT
I am going to fail my exam	I have an exam coming up	YES/NO	I am giving it my all, and that's what truly matters
I am unloveable	Everyone is loveable	YES/NO	I am a unique human being, one of a kind and I love myself
I am no good at maths	I am practising and learning maths	YES/NO	I am learning new things and I am kind to myself as I navigate this
I am scared I will fail	It's natural to feel scared of failure	YES/NO	I can learn from this experience, regardless of the outcome

The Inner Voice Exercise is a powerful tool to tackle and change our thoughts. When we question those thoughts, see how they might not be entirely accurate and adopt more positive views, we take control of our thinking. This process gives us a fresh perspective and a sense of empowerment, helps us step back from our thoughts and become more aware of our surroundings and how they influence them. With continued use of this tool, we'll experience a boost in our energy, more clarity in our thinking and a brighter outlook to help us face life's challenges.

Navigating Anxiety and Staying Present

The Awareness stage focuses on the importance of being fully present, connecting with reality and firmly grounding ourselves in the here and now. While we've already delved into how the Inner Voice Exercise can improve our grasp on reality, the question remains – how can we use awareness to ease the, sometimes, overwhelming impact of anxiety? Not only can anxiety sneak in during this stage, driven by worries about the past or future, but it also serves as a reminder of the work that lies ahead, and this realisation itself can trigger anxiety.

Let's look a little deeper into what anxiety actually is. Anxiety is a natural and often necessary human emotion. It's the body's way of responding to stress and alerting you to potential dangers. When you experience anxiety, your body releases a surge of adrenaline, commonly known as the 'fight-or-flight' response. This can be helpful in certain situations, like when you need to react quickly to a threat.

However, anxiety can become problematic when it is excessive, persistent or occurs without any apparent reason and starts to interfere with daily life and wellbeing. Common symptoms of anxiety include restlessness, muscle tension, racing thoughts, excessive worry, irritability and physical symptoms like sweating, trembling or a racing heart. It's essential to seek professional help if anxiety is significantly impacting your life. The tools explained in this chapter can be a helpful component in managing anxiety but are not a replacement for professional treatment.

How do we manage anxiety? For a start, it's crucial to show ourselves enormous amounts of self-compassion during these moments and practice grounding techniques the best we can. One effective method I developed to assist my clients in coping with anxiety is the BE SMART acronym, which involves various strategies for reconnecting with the present moment and can help navigate through challenging times. Here's a breakdown of the BE SMART acronym:

Claire

Meet Claire, a young lady who is an ocean lover and struggles with severe anxiety.

Claire was visibly trembling during our first meeting. Scheduling our initial session proved challenging, as her anxiety often felt overwhelming, making it difficult for her to engage with others. After a few cancellations, Claire finally committed to our session, she was obviously nervous, as she mentioned feeling hot, and her eyes were darting across the room when I tried to make eye contact.

In our conversation, Claire explained to me that she has a deep desire to participate more in life, particularly in activities she once loved but had abandoned due to her anxiety. Her love for ocean swimming was at the top of her list.

In the following sessions, we delved into the 'Inner Voice' Exercise, unravelling the origins of Claire's anxious thoughts. Providing her with a tool to understand and reframe these thoughts proved beneficial in reducing her anxiety. Claire discovered that her anxious thoughts echoed her mother's voice from her childhood, and she realised that the warnings her mother repeatedly emphasised, weren't necessarily useful in her current adult situation. As she learned to transform these thoughts into positive affirmations, that empowered rather than paralysed her, a sense of safety emerged, leading to a significant reduction in her anxiety.

With this progress, we transitioned to the next step: connecting with the present moment. Employing the BE SMART technique, Claire began to develop strategies for staying grounded in the now. By integrating the seven components of this technique into her daily routine, Claire gradually improved her ability to focus on the present moment. This instilled a sense of calm in her, preventing her thoughts from wandering into future scenarios. She felt more balanced and began to rediscover the joy of life as she used to know it. This encouraged her to return to the ocean where she reconnected with her love for being in the water, and her weekly swims started to become the highlight of her week again.

In the following sections, I'll briefly discuss the seven components of the BE SMART acronym, providing a quick overview of their benefits in anxiety reduction. While each component could be delved into extensively, the acronym aims to offer easily accessible tools during times of need. Therefore, we'll touch lightly on them in this book. However, I strongly encourage you to explore these components further if you find them beneficial for your wellbeing.

BE SMART

| Be Smart | Breath Exercise
Silence
Meditation
Art
Rest
Time in Nature |

Breath

Regulating your emotions can be swiftly achieved through the power of your breath. It acts as an in-built remote control for your nervous system; with slow, deep breaths, you can activate the parasympathetic nervous system, also known as your relaxation mode. This process brings about a sense of calm, reduces stress and lowers your heart rate. On the flip side, when we are anxious, we tend to take quick, shallow breaths which can trigger the sympathetic nervous system, which fuels the fight-or-flight response, making us feel more on edge. So, in a nutshell, your breath can be your best friend when dealing with anxiety.

One valuable technique I often recommend to my clients, especially those who are dealing with anxiety or panic attacks, is the '27 breaths' method. It involves counting down from 27 to 0, taking deliberate, slow breaths through your nose and focusing on the lowest part of your belly, while slowly counting down. Keep your awareness there with each breath in and out. Repeat if necessary. To enhance this practice and create a deeper sense of grounding, holding onto something, like a soft, comforting object, a favourite blanket or a fidget toy can be helpful. It's a simple and highly effective daily practice for calming the nerves and a valuable resource to keep within reach when dealing with a panic attack.

Exercise

While we are all probably familiar with the fact that exercise is beneficial for us, here are seven reasons why engaging in physical activity can also be helpful for managing anxiety. For Claire, picking up her daily exercise routine again was a life changer.

1. Stress Reduction: Physical activity triggers the release of endorphins, which are natural mood lifters. These 'feel-good' chemicals can help reduce stress, which is often a significant trigger for anxiety.
2. Cognitive Distraction: Engaging in exercise can divert your attention away from anxious thoughts and worries. Focusing on the physical demands of your workout can provide a mental break from anxiety.

3. Improved Sleep: Regular exercise can lead to better sleep quality. Quality sleep is essential for managing anxiety because sleep deprivation can exacerbate symptoms of anxiety.
4. Physical Health: Exercise can improve your overall physical health, this can help alleviate some of the physical symptoms often associated with anxiety, like muscle tension and restlessness.
5. Social Interaction: Participating in group exercise classes or team sports provides opportunities for social interaction, reducing feelings of isolation and loneliness, which are common triggers for anxiety.
6. Regulated Breathing: Many forms of exercise require controlled and deep breathing, which can mirror relaxation techniques like deep breathing exercises or meditation.
7. Endurance: Regular exercise can improve physical endurance, making your body better equipped to handle stress and anxiety, without becoming overwhelmed.

Silence

In our fast-paced, modern world, silence often seems like a rarity. We're constantly bombarded with noise, whether it's the sounds of traffic, the buzz of electronic devices or the chatter of our own minds. Yet, silence holds a remarkable therapeutic quality that can significantly benefit our mental and emotional wellbeing, particularly when it comes to reducing anxiety.

Constant noise creates a relentless sensory overload, contributing to increased stress and anxiety levels, which can keep our nervous systems on high alert. When we are on high alert, it can be difficult to find inner calm and peace. In contrast, silence offers a retreat from this sensory overload. By intentionally seeking out moments of silence, we can reduce this overstimulation and give our nervous systems a much-needed break, allowing us to reset and regain a sense of balance.

Silence isn't only the absence of sound, it's also an opportunity for self-reflection and mindfulness. In silent moments, we can tune into our thoughts, feelings and bodily sensations with greater clarity. For those dealing with anxiety, this can be transformative. It allows us to recognise anxious thought patterns and their triggers, and when we are more aware of our anxiety, we are also better equipped to address it effectively.

Moreover, silence is not only calming but also fosters creativity and problem-solving. By clearing the mental clutter, we make space for new ideas and approaches, which can help us find solutions and create positive change in our lives.

The power of silence is the power of presence. By actively seeking out silence and learning to appreciate its benefits, we can take steps towards reducing anxiety. In a world that rarely stops being quiet, the ability to find tranquillity within ourselves becomes a precious gift.

Meditation

Meditation serves as a powerful tool for reducing anxiety. When we meditate, we activate the relaxation response within our body, soothing the nervous system and reducing cortisol levels – the stress hormone linked to anxiety. It helps us access mindfulness, allowing us to observe our thoughts and emotions. As mentioned in Part 1, when we can pinpoint what we are feeling, it becomes much simpler to figure out the best way to address it. Through meditation, we can do this more easily and simultaneously achieve emotional regulation, which gives us greater stability and control over our reactions to stressors. When Claire started meditating, she felt more capable of examining her thoughts. By being still, practising deep breathing and meditating, she came to the realisation that the thoughts she was having on repeat were her memories of her mother's voice, warning her of danger. With that realisation, she applied the Inner Voice Exercise to gain more clarity and reshape her thoughts.

The practice of meditation also reduces symptoms like excessive worry and restlessness, helps improve sleep quality and addresses negative self-talk. The mind-body connection nurtured by meditation empowers us to attune to physical sensations, allowing us to better manage our anxiety responses.

Meditation offers a range of advantages for both mental and physical wellbeing. I encourage you to explore the various types of meditations available and discover what works best for your specific needs.

Art

Engaging in the creative journey of art can be a powerful and therapeutic experience, especially for those facing anxiety. The benefits are plenty, it provides relief from anxious thoughts and feelings and serves as an outlet for expressing complex emotions that are hard to put into words. As an Art Therapist, I've repeatedly witnessed the advantages my clients have gained from embracing the creative process. Beyond reducing anxiety, it positively impacts their overall wellbeing. They feel more liberated to be themselves and are inspired to participate in life; this happens for several reasons.

Firstly, exploring creativity helps us get unstuck. The way this works is that visual representations unlock a powerful way to release pent-up emotions and gain mental clarity. When we view our creations, we gain a fresh perspective, providing a new lens through which to understand our subconscious.

Whether it's drawing, painting or exploring other mediums, engaging in artistic pursuits promotes mindfulness and focus. The act of creation demands us to be present in the moment, grounding us, diverting our attention from anxiety inducing thoughts and calming the mind. But that is not all, art becomes a beautiful meditative process, naturally facilitating stress reduction and triggering our body's relaxation response. For Claire, the creative process became her sanctuary, where she would find respite from her restless mind and anxious thoughts. In these moments, she found peacefulness.

Completing an art project, regardless of its scale, gives us a sense of accomplishment and empowerment, contributing to a positive mindset. Few things are more fulfilling than finishing an art project and appreciating your creation, leaving you genuinely feeling good about yourself. Art also acts as a reflective space, offering insights into our emotions, self-awareness and understanding. Finally, art encourages personal exploration and experimentation without limitations, turning the canvas or medium into a space for freedom of self-discovery.

Whether this is facilitated by an art therapist, or a structured art group, or a spontaneous outlet, whether you are creating a masterpiece or just doodling on a scrap piece of paper, art can be a valuable and versatile tool for managing anxiety.

Rest

Rest plays an important role in reducing anxiety by providing our minds and bodies with the opportunity to recover from the daily stresses and demands of life. When we experience anxiety, our nervous system can become overstimulated, leading to heightened levels of tension and arousal. Rest acts as a reset button for our nervous system, allowing it to calm down and return to a state of balance.

Incorporating restful practices into our daily routine, such as getting an adequate amount of sleep, practising calming techniques like deep breathing or meditation and participating in leisurely activities that bring us joy and relaxation can help create a supportive environment for managing anxiety. Listening to our body and mind when they are asking for rest and taking the time to prioritise relaxation, allows us to recharge our batteries and experience a greater sense of tranquillity and clarity.

Rest is often an underestimated tool for managing anxiety. In our constantly busy and fast-paced society, there's the idea that resting is a luxury and that it can be perceived as being lazy or unproductive. However, rest is an essential part of our self-care. In fact, rest is not a luxury, it's a necessity and another valuable tool in reducing anxiety.

Nature

Being in nature offers numerous benefits for reducing anxiety and promoting overall mental wellbeing. One significant way nature achieves this is by lowering cortisol levels, the stress hormone. When we immerse ourselves in natural environments like forests, parks or beaches, the sights, sounds and smells of nature trigger a relaxation response in our bodies, helping to alleviate feelings of tension and anxiety. There is even a phenomenon known as 'nature deprivation' which refers to a lack of time spent in natural settings. Research has shown that this deprivation can have negative effects on our mental health, reminding us of the importance of finding time to be in nature.

Nature also encourages mindfulness and presence, inviting us to fully engage with the present moment. As we tune into the sights, sounds and sensations of the natural world, we can release worries about the past or future, grounding ourselves in the here and now. Whether it's a stroll in the park, a hike in the wilderness or simply sitting under a tree and listening to birdsong, spending time in nature makes us feel connected to the natural world and gives us a sense of something greater than ourselves. This connection can soothe the soul and calm the mind.

Incorporating the seven components of the BE SMART acronym into her daily routine proved transformative for Claire, it helped her be more present and reduced her anxiety. These accessible tools seamlessly integrated into her day-to-day life, gradually becoming habitual practices. Anticipating the feel-good endorphins and the peacefulness they brought, Claire looked forward to her routine, finding joy in its consistency.

The Awareness stage emphasises the importance of staying connected to the present moment and embracing reality fully. It encourages us to release resistance and denial, allowing us to confront the truth of our circumstances with honesty and openness. During this phase, we learn to reframe the negative inner dialogue and adopt a more positive perspective, enhancing our ability to grasp reality when fully present. With the clarity and insights gained through the Inner Voice Exercise and the BE SMART components, we, like Claire, can effectively reduce anxiety and better navigate challenging times.

In the next chapter, the Acceptance stage, we delve into letting go of resistance and practising self-acceptance, paving the way to regulate our emotions more effectively, releasing barriers and creating deeper connections within ourselves.

Remember our exploration of anxiety in Part 1, where we applied the SFUC method to comprehend our emotions. Now, let's revisit this section armed with our understanding of the Awareness stage. This may give us a clearer understanding of why anxiety is influencing our emotions in a specific manner. Feel free to respond to the Connect questions once more. As you engage with these questions, you'll likely discover that the more you inquire, the more effortlessly insights and connections unfold.

SFUC Method for Anxiety:

Stop: Take a deep breath

Feel: Ask yourself, "How am I feeling?"

Example: I am feeling restless, my heart is racing, I am breathing fast, I am feeling anxious.

Understand: Why am I feeling like this?

I am experiencing anxiety because my thoughts are about future events or scenarios. This hasn't happened yet, and I am most likely imagining a worst-case scenario.

Connect: Try answering the following questions:

1. How can I bring myself back to the present moment?
2. Is my current thought accurate?
3. How can I feel more grounded in this moment?

The Acceptance Stage

At the heart of this book is a fundamental concept – letting go of resistance and embracing exactly where we are. This is a crucial step on the path to wellbeing, a moment where we allow ourselves to be unapologetically authentic, even when faced with challenges. The act of letting go is not an easy one, but what if we could fully accept where we are, acknowledging our emotions and experiences without judgement or fear? It is in this space of self-acceptance that we can truly reconnect with ourselves.

Deep feelings of sadness can accompany this second stage as well as a sense of being stuck. Feeling stuck often signifies a challenge in propelling ourselves forward, taking action, and assuming accountability for the path ahead. The uncertainty of what lies ahead can be paralysing. This sense of being immobilised stems from the necessity of attaining a state of stillness. Yes, read that again – 'attaining a state of stillness'. It's essential to understand that this stillness serves a purpose. It provides the space to release what no longer serves us and allows us to process information, even grieve if necessary.

The feeling of being stuck will persist until we wholeheartedly embrace radical self-acceptance, self-compassion and self-care as we navigate this transformative process. This phase can be similar to a caterpillar within its cocoon, where changes slowly unfold. Just as a butterfly emerges beautifully after this process, our progression depends on whether we can fully embrace every part of the process and acknowledge that this transformation cannot be rushed.

In this chapter, we will explore the following tools: Self-care, Acceptance Meditation and the Pockets of Joy Exercise. These are designed to create space for stillness, cultivate self-compassion and work through the Acceptance stage to create feelings of contentment.

Janet

Meet Janet, who recently went through a divorce after being married for over two decades. The breakdown of the relationship rocked the foundation upon which her life was built. This left her completely bereaved and lost, unsure of how to pick up her life again. She felt overwhelmed by sadness and frustrated at her inability to move forward. She longed to build a new life in a different town but felt paralysed by the thought of leaving behind the home she had shared with her ex-husband for 20 years. Janet felt stuck in her sadness and struggled to take the next step forward.

During our sessions, I guided Janet through an exploration of the nature of sadness and the grieving process. I helped her understand that her feelings of sadness were a natural response to the significant life changes she had experienced. Together, we acknowledged that Janet was processing information that diverged from her expectations about how her life would unfold, leading to a sense of loss and disorientation. I emphasised that it was essential for Janet to allow herself to grieve fully for what she had lost before she could begin to plan a new path forward.

In addition to exploring grief, I introduced Janet to the concepts of self-compassion and self-care. I explained that during times of upheaval and transition, it was important for her to prioritise her own wellbeing and treat herself with kindness and understanding. I encouraged Janet to practice self-compassion by giving herself the same level of care and compassion she would offer to a dear friend facing similar challenges. Together, we discussed practical self-care strategies that Janet could incorporate into her daily routine.

Self-care

Self-care is a range of activities and practices aimed at preserving and improving our physical, emotional and mental wellbeing. It involves making deliberate choices to prioritise self-nurturing behaviours that promote overall health, particularly during times of stress or challenge.

Self-care activities can vary depending on individual preferences and needs but often include practices such as:

1. Physical self-care: Engaging in regular exercise, maintaining a balanced diet, getting enough sleep and practising good hygiene.
2. Emotional self-care: Identifying and expressing emotions in healthy ways, seeking support from friends, family or mental health professionals, practising self-compassion and acceptance and engaging in activities that bring joy and fulfilment.
3. Mental self-care: Cultivating mindfulness and relaxation techniques, setting boundaries to protect mental energy, engaging in stimulating activities such as learning new skills or hobbies and managing stress through techniques like deep breathing or journaling.
4. Social self-care: Nurturing relationships with supportive friends and family members, setting healthy boundaries in relationships, seeking out social activities that bring joy and connection and minimising exposure to draining social situations.

5. Spiritual self-care: Connecting with one's values, beliefs or sense of purpose, engaging in spiritual practices such as meditation, prayer or spending time in nature and fostering a sense of inner peace and fulfilment.

Overall, self-care involves intentionally prioritising activities and practices that promote wellbeing across all aspects of life, to help us better cope with life's challenges.

For Janet, self-care post-divorce involved, going for regular walks on her favourite beach, journaling to process her emotions and enjoying long lunches with supportive friends who brought comfort and laughter into her life.

Janet also learned the importance of setting boundaries and saying no to social commitments that drained her energy and left her feeling worse. Instead, choosing activities and interactions that made her feel nurtured and accepted at exactly where she was emotionally. From this standpoint, she could acknowledge the changes in her life and the grief for what she had lost and explore her emotions linked to her future path. I introduced her to the 'Acceptance Meditation', providing her with the space to address the emotions hindering her progress, allowing her to process them and find a path forward at her own pace when she felt ready.

Below, you will find the 'Acceptance meditation'. Use this meditation whenever you feel stuck or need to embrace the process of acceptance. It can help you find peace with your current situation and provide a sense of clarity and calm.

The Acceptance Meditation

In this meditation, inspired by the essence of letting go and embracing our current state, we focus on being kind to ourselves, offering self-compassion in moments of challenge and pain. We grant ourselves permission to face our emotions head-on. Whether it's grief, uncertainty or simply feeling stuck, it's all welcomed with open arms. This is a space where there is no judgement and where self-acceptance begins.

Find a quiet, peaceful moment for yourself. Sit or lie down, gently close your eyes and let the outside world fade away. Take a deep breath, and as you exhale, begin to release the tension and resistance that may reside within you. Picture a soft, warm light surrounding you, expanding with each breath, creating a sense of safety, openness and acceptance.

With each breath, invite a feeling of peace and acceptance. It's perfectly okay to be precisely where you are at this moment, with all your thoughts and emotions. Allow yourself to be fully present, free from self-judgement.

As you continue to breathe deeply, visualise a gentle stream of tranquillity flowing over you, carrying away any resistance or expectations. Be open to whatever thoughts or emotions arise within you. Release the need to be anyone other than your genuine self.

This is where you confront your losses, your grief. Sit with them, acknowledging their presence. It's alright to feel this sadness and hold it close until you're ready to let it go. In time, you'll surrender, not with resistance, but with acceptance.

You might feel stuck in this phase, and that's perfectly okay. Embrace this moment with deep self-compassion, understanding that healing takes time. It's in this space where you can let go. Believe in yourself and your immense capacity for healing. When you're ready, you'll assume full responsibility for yourself and recognise the areas where you can create opportunities for change. Take a few more deep breaths, appreciating the space you are creating for yourself, to be you and the strength you carry within. When you feel ready, slowly open your eyes, bringing with you a sense of acceptance and self-compassion.

In Janet's case, the 'Acceptance Meditation' gave her a space to explore acceptance and embrace her current state with unapologetic authenticity. In this compassionate environment, she could fully connect with her feelings and release any lingering resistance. This allowed for a deeper connection with herself and opened up greater opportunities for healing.

Next, we introduced the 'Pockets of Joy' exercise. By identifying simple pleasures that brought her joy and incorporating them into her daily routine, Janet began to experience more positivity in her life.

The Pockets of Joy Exercise

The Pockets of Joy Exercise offers a simple yet powerful method for infusing our lives with moments of joy. The concept is straightforward: identify the simple things that bring you joy and incorporate them into your life as much as you can. These 'pockets' of joy act as reserves, ready to be accessed whenever needed, providing instant upliftment.

Here's how it works:

1. Identify your pockets of joy: Take some time to reflect on the experiences, activities or sensations that bring you joy. These could be simple pleasures from your past or present that ignite a sense of happiness within you. Consider moments from your childhood or times when you felt truly alive and carefree.
2. Make a list: Write down at least five things that bring you joy or used to bring you joy. These can be anything from swinging on a swing to feeling the sunshine on your face, listening to your favourite music, spending time with loved ones or engaging in hobbies like gardening or playing music. Be specific and choose activities that resonate deeply with you.
3. Create your joy reserve: Once you've identified your pockets of joy, find ways to integrate them into your daily life if you can. This could involve scheduling time for these activities, keeping reminders in

your environment or making space for spontaneous moments of joy. Consider creating a physical 'joy reserve' by writing your pockets of joy on slips of paper and placing them in your actual pocket or in a jar where you can easily access them.
4. Access your pockets of joy during challenging times or when you're feeling sad. Reach into your joy reserve and select a pocket of joy to lift your spirits. Whether it's taking a walk in nature, enjoying a sunrise or reading a good book, allow yourself to fully experience this moment and the joy it brings.

By creating a collection of pockets of joy, we can empower ourselves to navigate difficult times, work through feelings of sadness and cultivate contentment.

Embracing True Acceptance for Social Freedom

In this chapter so far, we have delved into the concept of acceptance – shedding resistance and giving ourselves the time to embrace our current state. Allowing unapologetic authenticity, even amid challenges. We explored how, in this compassionate space, we can genuinely reconnect with ourselves. When we feel like we can be ourselves, we can express ourselves better and connect with others more easily. This is an expression of social freedom.

The Acceptance stage and social freedom go hand in hand, together they can create a nurturing environment characterised by understanding, empathy and support. When we authentically accept ourselves and others, we are establishing a space where belonging and authenticity flourish. This acceptance in social interactions becomes the cornerstone for people to feel valued, fostering positive connections and relationships. It sets the stage for a supportive community where everyone can freely express themselves without the fear of judgement.

In the context of mental health, acceptance assumes a critical role. It can be extremely empowering and comforting when someone recognises and embraces your current state without the burden of societal expectations. This compassionate approach fuels personal growth and healing. Creating a safe space for authenticity, as opposed to criticising, dismissing or shaming, which leads to further separation and isolation. As acceptance becomes an integral part of social freedom, it empowers people to navigate their unique journey at their own pace, fostering a culture of inclusivity and understanding, while simultaneously breaking down barriers surrounding mental health challenges.

When it comes to our Wellbeing Cup and the seven stages, we can be supportive of others as they work through their stages as well. When supporting someone through a difficult time, it is essential to start with understanding and accepting the stage they are at in their healing journey. Most of us cherish those moments when someone truly sees us, making us feel valued and loved and instilling hope for a positive future. From this place of no judgement and loving kindness, we can stand by ready to help navigate the next stage. When we offer this kind of support with care, we can ensure it aligns with the individual's readiness for the next stage. Attempting to rush someone to a stage we believe they should be at may backfire, leading them to feel misunderstood or like a failure. Think of a caterpillar going through a transformation in its cocoon. Some things can't be rushed. Each person's wellbeing journey unfolds at its own pace and pushing someone into something they are not ready for can result in setbacks. Real acceptance involves meeting them at their current stage and providing assistance tailored to their unique needs. This approach ensures a more empathetic and realistic form of support – this, in essence, embodies true acceptance.

Emilia

Take Emilia's story, for instance. She's a young adult who faced some tough times during her teenage years, getting caught up in heavy drug use and becoming addicted. This led her to drop out of school, and she spent years struggling with her mental health, resulting in being admitted to facilities for months at a time. Recently, she's made progress in overcoming her addiction and is living at home with her parents, rebuilding her life.

She is slowly coming to terms with the damage the addiction has done to her body and mind, as it has left her with a mental disorder and physical health issues as well. Emilia is grappling with intense sadness and grief for the lost years and the person she used to be. She is also coming to terms with the pain and dysfunction her addiction has caused her family and other relationships (Acceptance Stage).

She realises that drugs were a way to numb her emotions in the past, so she didn't feel uncomfortable. Now she is taking accountability and finding ways to work through these emotions in a healthy way (Accountability stage). Her aim is to have a part-time job, but she struggles to stay in a job for long due to insecurities and a feeling of not belonging. This leads to her feeling upset with herself for quitting and not trying harder (Empowerment Stage).

Her family struggles to understand this and has often expressed their frustration with her for not keeping a job or not going back to school so she can finish her schooling and get a more suitable job. They also want her to try independent living so she can build her own life (Action Stage). They say they feel disconnected from her, as the more they try to help and suggest things to her, the more she hides away in her room, complaining that she feels overwhelmed and to leave her alone.

Emilia is in the Acceptance stage and is trying to make her way into the Accountability stage. At this point, she needs time to grieve for what she has lost in the years her addiction consumed her. She also needs to feel more balanced and worthy of herself before she can overcome her feelings of insecurity that stop her from taking action to find a suitable job or live on her own. Her family would like to see her in the Action Stage, but their well-meant intentions are causing her to feel misunderstood and like a failure, prompting her to hide away in her room, away from a world where she feels she can't be herself. She does not feel accepted.

The Acceptance stage is a courageous acknowledgement of one's current reality. It is not a surrender to circumstances; rather, it is an act of empowerment. It signifies a conscious decision to face the truth, fostering a foundation for personal growth and healing. There is no room for avoidance and denial anymore. Just as Janet recognised the need to grieve and work through her emotions, for Emilia this stage provides an essential pause for self-compassion and assessment.

During the Acceptance Stage, people often grapple with complex emotions, ranging from grief and regret to the gradual emergence of accountability. It serves as a bridge between past struggles and future possibilities, laying the groundwork for subsequent stages of accountability, empowerment and action.

Recall our exploration of the emotion of sadness in Part 1, where we applied the SFUC method. Now, let's revisit this section armed with our understanding of the Acceptance Stage.

SFUC Method for Sadness:

Stop: Take a deep breath

Feel: Take a moment to ask yourself, "How am I feeling?"

Example: I am feeling flat and empty. I feel like crying. I am feeling sad.

Understand: Why am I feeling like this?

I'm dealing with information that doesn't match my desired outcome. While I'm trying to come to terms with it, I'm also feeling a sense of loss, and this is making me sad.

Connect: Try answering the following questions:

1. Is it possible for me to embrace my current situation and accept the feelings that arise?
2. Is it possible for me to practice self-compassion for the loss I am experiencing?
3. Are there little moments of joy I can discover every day?
4. What matters most to me that I can connect with to boost my positivity and sense of fulfilment?
5. Have I established a self-care routine that I can rely on when I feel like this?

The Accountability Stage

As we gradually move beyond the Acceptance stage, where we practised letting go of what no longer serves us and embracing self-compassion as a cocoon for self-reflection, we step into the Accountability stage. Being accountable means taking ownership of our behaviour when we are completely transparent with ourselves. It means taking responsibility for the outcomes of our choices with integrity and deciding which problems are ours to solve and which are not.

Instead of blaming others when things go wrong, we look inside ourselves and ask how to improve things. It's about learning from tough times and empowering ourselves to navigate challenges. This shift allows us to transform moments of upset into opportunities for personal growth and resilience. By taking accountability, we recognise our role in creating positive change and create space to regulate emotions, communicate effectively and set boundaries to navigate challenges with clarity.

Embracing accountability is closely tied to the mindful allocation of our energy. Our energy holds immense value, serving as the driving force behind how we feel about ourselves. In this chapter, we delve into strategies to help channel this precious energy effectively, especially in a world where it's easy to feel off balance. The key aspects we explore include fostering clear communication within ourselves and others, establishing healthy boundaries and nurturing resilience. By following these steps, we pave the way for a more accountable and balanced life.

Bursting the Bubble

To fully embrace accountability and welcome growth and possibility, it's essential to have faith in our capabilities and resist the tendency to play small. Playing small involves downplaying our abilities and potential. Breaking free from this pattern and unlocking our full potential requires addressing and understanding the underlying factors. This takes self-reflection, releasing negative inner chatter, redirecting our energy and cultivating our inner resilience. It means moving beyond the comfort we may gain from staying small and to stop distracting ourselves from the awareness that we have unrealised potential.

Picture this: a bubble that wraps around you, created not by soap and water but by the constant hum of negative inner chatter. It's the commentary in your mind that keeps you stuck, whispers self-doubt and maintains the status quo. This bubble, although invisible, is a powerful force shaping your thoughts, feelings and actions.

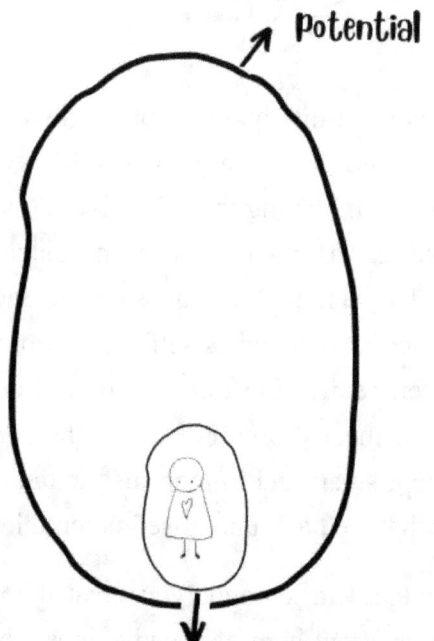

the bubble that keeps you stuck through negative inner chatter

Breaking free from this confining bubble requires a conscious effort to pop it. Negative inner chatter often stems from a desire to protect ourselves, but in reality, it confines us to a limited version of who we are meant to be.

Alex

Meet Alex, a highly intelligent and professionally successful young man, with a friendly and likeable appearance. Despite

his outward success, Alex has struggled with a persistent sense of being an outsider and experiences difficulty connecting with people. This struggle originates from a history of bullying during his school years, which left a lasting impact on his social interactions.

As a coping mechanism, Alex withdraws from group activities and chooses to spend extended periods alone, burying himself in work and building a successful business. Despite his busyness, he experiences feelings of loneliness and often gets upset. His ultimate goal is to participate in his community, find his tribe and establish lasting friendships. However, when attempting to connect with others, Alex is overwhelmed by a constant negative inner chatter, fearing that people will perceive him poorly. This mental struggle exhausts him even before leaving the house and often leads him to decide that it's better to stay home where he feels safe.

In our conversations, Alex often shares that in his daily interactions with the people close to him, he goes above and beyond to help others, even when it makes him uncomfortable – exhibiting people-pleasing tendencies. Motivated by a desire to be perceived as the 'nice guy', he rarely communicates his true feelings or frustrations directly. Instead, he tends to suppress them, continuing to accommodate others. Deep down, there's a fear that expressing his anger might make him unlikeable, leading to anger and resentment when others don't return the support he offers. He channels his anger by engaging with online gaming platforms anonymously. This pattern leaves Alex exhausted, lacking motivation to make connections and finding it difficult to engage with the outside world.

Throughout our sessions, we focused on ways for Alex to embrace a more authentic and liberated version of himself, by equipping him with strategies to preserve his energy and set healthy boundaries that support his wellbeing.

Managing Our Energy Mindfully

In the 'Awareness Stage' chapter, we engaged in challenging and transforming our thoughts to embrace more positive perspectives. As you apply this tool, you might experience a surge in your energy. Now, in this chapter, we're taking it a step further, focusing on harnessing our energy to foster a positive self-feeling. How can you tap into this energy? To start, let's examine where we're unintentionally letting precious energy slip.

When it comes to managing our energy, mindfulness is crucial. Our energy is a valuable resource, and how we use it significantly impacts our wellbeing. Ever find yourself asking, "Why am I always tired? Why do I get upset so easily?" It might be time to examine where your energy is going, because the 'leaking of energy' is a constant drain on our energetic wellbeing. This can leave us feeling depleted with feelings of fatigue, upset and resentment.

Protecting our energetic wellbeing can be hard, especially in a culture that prioritises constant activity over mindful presence. As a result of this, recognising when we are out of balance and depleted has become a challenge. The focus on being busy DO-ing, has overshadowed the importance of simply BE-ing. Unfortunately, we've become so accustomed to the relentless pursuit of tasks and goals that we've forgotten what it feels like to just be. The constant engagement with DO-ing becomes problematic when it becomes an escape or distraction, keeping us from addressing the core issue of not reaching our full potential. This hinders us from taking complete responsibility and accountability for our situation.

Let's be completely transparent with ourselves for a minute – where do we feel we are unbalanced and leaking precious energy? Identifying this is the first step towards authentic accountability. As illustrated in the examples below, we lose precious energy through our energy 'gaps' when we engage in certain activities.

Intentionally BE-ing

When we are aware of the energy gaps, we can take deliberate steps to safeguard our emotional and energetic boundaries. This is essential for maintaining a positive and healthier state – referred to as BE-ing. This state is characterised by stability, peace and balance. As we consciously relocate our energy and close the gaps, clarity emerges, revealing the necessary steps to improve our emotional wellbeing and unlocking the key to stability. It also shines a spotlight on anything that is not a good fit anymore for our newfound energy. We become more selective and protective of what makes us feel good and what doesn't.

Energy Vampires

When we are intentional in our BE-ing, we become more aware of the dynamics of our interactions, enabling us to recognise and address potential energy-draining situations. Certain social interactions hold the power to shape our energetic wellbeing, either uplifting or depleting it. In the presence of energy gaps, we unfortunately make ourselves more susceptible to the influence of energy vampires.

An 'energy vampire' is a term often used to describe someone who drains the energy, vitality or positivity of those around them. These people may behave in a way that leaves others feeling emotionally exhausted, depleted or negatively impacted. Energy vampires can include people who are constantly negative, critical or demanding, as well as those who thrive on drama or consistently bring a sense of heaviness to interactions. You may be thinking of someone you know by now and wondering what to do about it? Good question.

Let's start with addressing the aspect of setting boundaries with others, as it is a huge component in taking accountability to protect our energy.

Safeguarding Your Energy Through Emotional Boundaries

Reflecting on the insights from Part 1 of this book, we delved into the emotion of upset as well as feelings of resentment, anger and distress. Upset often arises from a situation not in alignment with our expectations or a sense of misunderstanding or unfair treatment, either towards ourselves or those we care about. As we transition from the constant activity of DO-ing to the intentional inward focus of BE-ing, a natural outcome is heightened awareness and accountability for our words and actions.

This shift can be both revealing and challenging, potentially triggering emotional responses and upsets not only within ourselves but also those around us. So, it is very likely, that in the complex dance of human connections, we'll experience moments of upset at some point. Effective communication and establishing emotional boundaries play important roles in regulating our emotions and, at the same time, nurturing healthy relationships.

Emotional boundaries empower you to safeguard your energy, articulate your needs clearly and create an environment of mutual respect. Without clear boundaries, others may not realise the toll things are taking on you, therefore it is important to establish and communicate your limits for a more genuine relationship with them and yourself. Below, you'll find a few practical examples to guide you in this practice.

If these examples seem challenging, I suggest trying to practice in front of a mirror or with someone you trust until you feel more comfortable.

Express Your Needs Clearly:

Clear communication of your needs is essential for effective and healthy relationships. Expressing your needs with clarity helps prevent misunderstandings that could lead to hurt, anger, resentment or confusion.

Examples:

- "I would like some alone time."
- "I need space right now."
- "I require more time to focus on my work."

Establish Limits:

Clarity about your limits fosters a sense of respect and understanding in relationships.

Examples:

- "I'm not comfortable discussing this topic."
- "For this, I only have limited time available."
- "I won't tolerate disrespectful behaviour. But when you can be respectful, we can revisit this conversation."

Assertive Communication:

Being assertive is a valuable skill that allows you to express your thoughts clearly, explain your perspective, enhance your self-esteem and earn the respect of others.

Examples:

- "I feel overwhelmed when you raise your voice, so please speak to me calmly."

- "I value our friendship, but I can't continue like this if you don't respect my boundaries."
- "I have a different perspective on this, and I'd like you to respect that."

Set Consequences:

Clearly defined consequences help reinforce the importance of respecting boundaries and highlight the accountability of the people involved.

Examples:

- "If you continue to interrupt me during work, I'll need to find a quieter place to focus."
- "For me to work here to my best abilities, I will need a consistent routine, so I can do my job well."
- "If you disrespect my boundaries, I may need to distance myself for a while."

Use 'I' Statements:

'I' statements allow for expressions of concerns, feelings and needs without placing blame on others or sounding threatening. It is an effective way to communicate one's perspective without causing the listener to shut down or become defensive.

Examples:

- "I need to prioritise my health/work/family time right now, so I can't commit to additional responsibilities."

- "I feel uncomfortable when my personal space is invaded, so I'd appreciate it if you could respect that."
- "I value our time together, but I'm feeling overwhelmed, and I need to reschedule our plans."

Be Firm but Polite:

Firmness communicates the seriousness of your boundaries, while politeness reflects your value for the relationship and your intention to maintain a positive interaction. This balanced approach ensures effective communication while respecting the dynamics of the relationship.

Examples:

- "I appreciate your invitation, but I have to decline at this time."
- "I'd like to help, but I have to prioritise myself/my own wellbeing right now."
- "I appreciate your interest in my work, but I can't commit to that at the moment."

Express Your Feelings:

Expressing our feelings enhances our ability to connect with others. When we openly communicate our emotions, it creates a bridge for understanding and empathy.

Examples:

- "I feel anxious when there's too much pressure on me, so I need to set this boundary."

- "I'm concerned about how I may react, so I need to take a step back."
- "I feel angry and I need space to think."
- "I feel overwhelmed, and I need to prioritise self-care."

Setting boundaries is an act of self-respect and a cornerstone for nurturing relationships. It also involves staying consistent in enforcing these boundaries and remaining open to discussions about them when necessary. The journey to safeguarding your energy begins with clear communication and a commitment to your wellbeing.

Nurturing Resilience

Resilience is the ability to adapt and bounce back from life's challenges and setbacks. It is not only a quality but a practice, cultivated through commitment, accountability and the ability to draw on past successes. In the face of uncertainty, resilience is a powerful tool for navigating life's complexities.

Remember Claire from a few chapters ago and her struggles with anxiety? She started using the BE SMART method, incorporating daily swims to help her connect to the present moment. By staying committed to her ocean swims, Claire experienced a shift that extended far beyond the swimming, she was experiencing the transformative power of commitment and resilience. By prioritising this daily commitment, a ripple effect began, influencing her ability to keep other commitments – she even started training for swimming competitions. She embraced all weather conditions. Rain, wind and cold became mere challenges to overcome, increasing her confidence so she could overcome difficulties. This resilience spilled over into her social life, where she now felt comfortable attending lunches with friends, who in turn, began to feel inspired by her dedication, which made her feel empowered. The energy she once spent worrying about the future and other people's opinions was now redirected towards building resilience within herself.

She leaned on this newfound inner strength when her mother became very ill. The illness heightened her anxiety, but instead of getting lost in the turmoil, she remained steadfast, stuck to her routine and became a great support for her mother. This experience not only reinforced her resilience but also empowered her to know that she could navigate challenging times.

Claire's story highlights the concept of a 'resilience bank'. Each time she successfully held herself accountable, it became a deposit in her resilience account. This accumulation of successes empowered her during tough times and the memory of past successes guided her to see opportunities for growth in difficult times. It was a reminder that she could create positive change by staying accountable and drawing from her resilience.

The Resilience Bank

Moving beyond the Acceptance Stage, uncertainty about the way forward is common, and taking accountability can feel overwhelming. To start the process, building up resilience in the resilience bank can be a good starting point. This involves managing two accounts: the Everyday Account and the Savings Account.

The Everyday Account is where we stop playing small and actively seek opportunities to build up our resilience through daily or regular practices. It's a space where we consistently deposit small, regular efforts to strengthen our ability to face challenges.

On the other hand, the Savings Account is reserved for difficult times. Here, we find opportunities for personal growth during tough circumstances. This dual-account approach gives us a strategy to develop and use resilience in various ways.

The Everyday Account

- Stop playing small and redirect your energy to Be-ing

- Actively seek opportunities and embrace new experiences

- Challenge yourself with tasks or activities beyond your usual comfort zone

- Strive for a positive outcome by persevering

- Recognize and celebrate your achievements, no matter how small

- Feel empowered from achievements and navigating challenges

- Accumulate resilience for Savings Account

The Savings Account

- In times of upset or difficulty, draw from the resilience accumulated in the Everyday Account

- Use past successes and experiences in navigating challenges

- View challenging situations as opportunities to learn and build more resilience

- Embrace difficulties as a chance for personal growth

- Actively create positive change through your actions

- Positive change becomes a powerful tool for regulating your emotions (SFUC method)

- Create boundaries as protective measures, preventing energy depletion and maintaining emotional balance

As you can see, building resilience through the Everyday Account involves actively seeking opportunities and engaging in daily practices that result in positive outcomes that make us feel empowered. While in the Savings Account, we draw on the accumulated strength from the Everyday account to create our present action, generating opportunities to further our growth and regulate our emotions. By using both our accounts in this way, taking accountability becomes not just a response to challenges, but an ongoing practice that enhances resilience and our self-worth.

In the upcoming chapter, we will delve into the connection between accountability and our core values and how it paves the path to the transformative process of empowerment.

Recall our exploration of the emotion of Upset in Part 1, where we applied the SFUC method. Now, let's revisit this section armed with our understanding of the Accountability stage.

SFUC Method for Upset:

Stop: Take a deep breath.

Feel: Take a moment to ask yourself, "How am I feeling?"

Example: I am so upset this happened. I feel like I am going to burst, I am so angry. My heart is beating fast, and I feel like yelling loudly.

Understand: Why am I feeling like this?

I'm experiencing anger because I believe something didn't unfold as it should have, or someone's behaviour seemed inappropriate from my perspective. This left me feeling as if I, or someone I care about, wasn't treated respectfully or fairly.

Connect: Try answering the following questions:

1. Is what I am feeling based on solid evidence, or am I making assumptions? What are the concrete facts?
2. Can I take a step back and view this from a wider perspective? Am I feeling distressed about the current situation, or does this somehow trigger memories of past experiences?
3. Is it necessary for me to establish stronger boundaries in this situation?
4. What steps can I take to improve communication in this situation?
5. Am I becoming entangled in matters that aren't my responsibility? How can I narrow my focus to what truly concerns me, take responsibility for my role, redirect my energy and initiate positive changes if possible?

The Empowerment Stage

The Empowerment stage is where the efforts of accountability blossom into freedom and control over our lives. It's a transformative stage that requires a strong belief that we are capable of making changes and prioritising a life that supports our wellbeing.

Believing in oneself is at the core of empowerment, and despite feelings of insecurity, we can break through the barriers to build a strong foundation of self-belief. In this stage, we also acknowledge how far we have come on our journey, recognising our strengths and cultivating a deep sense of worthiness. From here, guided by a connection to our values, we embrace our true selves and life begins to flow.

As we move into the Empowerment Stage, let's take a moment to reflect on our journey so far.

Our exploration began in the Awareness Stage, where we developed the skill of staying present, shedding denial and distractions. We focused on the issues brought to our attention, recognising our thoughts and carefully examining them.

In the Acceptance Stage, we embraced the wisdom of taking our time. Whatever surfaced during this stage, was met with patience. We navigated the transformation process, allowing ourselves to feel and process emotions like grief and sadness. Resistance was released, making space for us to lean into discomfort.

The Accountability Stage saw us rolling up our sleeves, taking control and assuming responsibility for the changes we aimed to bring about. Pushing through, even when we felt extremely uncomfortable, we recognised that our body and mind needed us to take charge, and taking ownership and responsibility became our allies. This demanded serious dedication and resilience, reminding us of the power we have to shape our future. This power, unique and deeply connected to your true being, is a force that, when harnessed, has the potential to create incredible forward movement, paving the way to construct the life you desire.

Now, as we enter the Empowerment Stage, our Wellbeing Cup is halfway full, and we carry the lessons and strength gained with us. Every success and moment of resilience we've experienced has laid the groundwork for this next chapter.

Breaking through the Barriers

Navigating the path to shape our future isn't always a walk in the park; challenges and discomfort may arise along the way. Therefore, as we transition into the Empowerment Stage, it's important to keep up with the regular check-ins we discussed in the Accountability Stage. These check-ins are like a reference point, ensuring we stay on the right path and don't slip back into playing small, which can be a familiar but limiting habit.

During times of transition, it is natural to want to retreat to familiar comforts, especially as we begin to step into the spotlight. However, resisting the temptation to go back to playing small is important. Understandably, slipping back into old habits may briefly feel comforting, but deep down, we know that it's not helpful for our growth. Moreover, with each refusal to revert to those old patterns, we reinforce our commitment to progress, building more resilience, and over time, what once felt uncomfortable, becomes our new comfort zone.

As we partake in this journey, our lives change, and it's common to encounter feelings of insecurity along the way. While these emotions may initially seem daunting, they serve as indicators of our growth and transformation. Rather than viewing them as setbacks, we can reframe them as stepping stones guiding us towards positive shifts. They signify our progress as we break through barriers and embrace an empowered version of ourselves.

Feeling Insecure

Insecurity is a deep-seated feeling of uncertainty, self-doubt or a lack of confidence in oneself and one's abilities. It often stems from a fear of not meeting certain standards, a belief of not being good enough or concerns about how others perceive us. This emotion can significantly impact different aspects of life, including relationships, work and personal achievements.

When dealing with insecurities, we may frequently seek validation from others, experience anxiety about our performance or appearance and a persistent fear of rejection or judgement. These feelings can be related to past experiences, trauma or societal expectations that contribute to a negative self-perception.

Insecurity can also manifest through certain behaviours like bragging, appearing superior, expressing strong opinions, being overly clingy or seeking constant reassurance. This behaviour is closely linked to one's sense of self-worth, an internal acknowledgement of being worthy and deserving of love from oneself and others.

No one enjoys feeling insecure, as it tends to push us into playing small, limiting our potential and preventing us from pursuing our desires. Understanding how to improve our self-worth becomes the main factor in letting go of those feelings of insecurity that often hold us back. Alex's journey serves as an example of how increasing self-worth can help us break through that barrier.

Remember Alex from the previous chapter and how he struggles with feeling like an outsider and experiences difficulty connecting with people? In Alex's case, the bullying he endured during his school years left deep emotional scars, shaping his perception of himself and influencing how he believes others see him.

Being called names like 'freak' during his school years had a lasting effect on Alex, even though he recognises now that those labels were not a true reflection of who he is. The emotional wounds from that time continue to affect him as an adult. The persistent sense of being an outsider and difficulty connecting with people still make him feel deeply insecure.

Alex bravely shared his struggles with socialising, revealing the deep feelings of shame that often overcame him. Out of fear of judgement, he would cover himself up with oversized clothing and sunglasses and often stand behind objects, trying to create a shield between himself and the world.

In the due course of our sessions, we worked on understanding the difference between self-esteem and self-worth and shifting the focus from external validation to internal recognition. Alex discovered that by placing the focus on his self-worth, he could gain a degree of control over his emotional wellbeing, and by acknowledging and nurturing what made him unique, Alex could see value within himself. This internal shift allowed him to control and enhance his self-worth, a big step forward in his journey towards social freedom.

Self-worth

Before we delve into the exploration of self-worth, let's examine what differentiates it from self-esteem, as these terms often intertwine but have separate meanings.

Self-esteem refers to how you perceive and feel about yourself in various situations. It can fluctuate based on your mood, performance, circumstances or the opinions and approval of others. In simpler terms, self-esteem is like a dynamic barometer that measures your confidence and self-perception at a specific moment.

For example, if you achieve a personal goal, your self-esteem might soar. On the flip side, a setback or criticism could temporarily lower your self-esteem. It's influenced by external factors and can vary throughout different experiences.

Below are a few examples of external factors that can influence your self-esteem:

- Your strengths and weaknesses that you focus on the most.
- The feedback you receive from others, both positive and negative.
- Your general mood, stress levels and emotional states.
- Social comparisons, the tendency to measure yourself against others.
- The realisation of goals or the disappointment of unmet expectations.

- The lens through which you interpret your experiences and make sense of your identity.

On the other hand, self-worth is a more foundational aspect of your self-perception. It's a stable understanding of your value and who you are as a person. Unlike self-esteem, which can be influenced by external factors and fluctuates, your self-worth remains more constant, providing a steady foundation that isn't easily shaken by external circumstances. It's about recognising and believing in your worthiness as an individual, regardless of the ups and downs of daily life.

People with high self-worth:

- Feel deserving of love and respect from others.
- Believe in their goodness, worthiness and lovability.
- Treat themselves with self-compassion, kindness and respect.
- Embrace and love themselves without conditions or exceptions.
- Belief in their potential for growth, change and improvement.
- Acknowledge their flaws and accept that making mistakes is a natural part of the human experience.
- Recognise that mistakes do not threaten their core identity or sense of worth, instead, they become opportunities for learning and growth.

You may wonder if you can improve your self-esteem through self-worth. The key to that answer lies in understanding and nurturing our authentic selves. Let's circle back to what we talked about in our last chapter. Often, we find that self-esteem is dependent on external factors, such as achievements, successes and the approval of others also known as DO-ing. On the other side, self-worth is about acknowledging and embracing our intrinsic value and is deeply rooted in intentional BE-ing. This shift in focus from DO-ing to BE-ing is where we need to go to foster a deep sense of value within. When we prioritise intentional BE-ing, the need for high self-esteem disappears, as our worth no longer depends on external validations, instead, we feel worthy of who we are.

People with high self-worth believe in their potential for growth and have an understanding that no matter what circumstance they are in, they are always loveable and worthy as they are. Remember how in previous chapters, we talked about practising self-compassion and acceptance? They build the foundation for a deep sense of self-worth, so does being aware of our energy gaps and practising intentional BE-ing. So, armed with that knowledge, we now can further explore and examine our core identity.

Shame and Its Impact on Self-worth

For Alex, socialising became weighed down with his feelings of shame. The fear of being judged or perceived negatively by others created a heavy burden that affected his ability to engage with the world. He deeply felt that he did not belong around others, convinced there was something wrong with him. The weight of this shame prompted him to adopt a physical disguise, a shield to protect himself from the imagined criticisms of those around him. Deep down he agreed with the criticism, as he saw himself as unacceptable to be around. His vision of himself and the world around him had become distorted, and disguising himself made it easier for him to deal with those complex emotions.

Shame is a complex and deeply ingrained emotion that shapes our perception of self and our interactions with the world. It's more than just a passing feeling; it's the internalisation of experiences that clash with our values, leaving a mark on our sense of worth. This painful emotion is connected to negative self-beliefs and the pervasive feeling that something is inherently wrong with us, fostering a sense of inadequacy.

For Alex, the perception of being 'likeable and a good person' are personal values that carry immense importance. Therefore, the bullying he experienced in his school years impacted him deeply. He internalised the experiences and they significantly influenced how he felt about himself, making him believe he was a freak that no one wanted to be around.

One of the challenges with shame is how it warps our reality. Instead of recognising that something bad happened to us when we are dealing with shame, we often believe we are fundamentally bad. This distorted perspective compels us to hide, play small, withdraw and harshly judge ourselves, fostering feelings of inadequacy, insecurity and an unwarranted belief that we are not good enough or deserving of love and connection. These energy-draining behaviours hinder us from simply being ourselves, trapping us in a cycle that takes us away from authentic living.

Shame can manifest in various everyday behaviours, significantly influencing our actions. These behaviours may include perfectionism, struggles with body image, a tendency to keep quiet, isolation and self-destructive tendencies. The presence of shame is most notable in the Awareness, Acceptance and Accountability Stages of our journey. As we move forward into the Empowerment Stage, there is an opportunity to break free from its constraining grip.

Overcoming shame requires a shift in our approach, moving from a stance of self-protection to one of vulnerability. This involves expressing shame through appropriate responses. An important aspect of this process involves practising self-compassion, wherein we consciously acknowledge and embrace our experiences with loving kindness towards ourselves. It's important to remind ourselves that past experiences don't change our worth as individuals; we are always worthy of love and connection, regardless of what we have been through.

Remember 'The Voice in the Head' exercise from the Awareness Stage? When dealing with shameful feelings, this can be a powerful tool to help us identify and challenge the negative self-talk associated with our self-worth, creating a more compassionate internal dialogue. Additionally, the 'Acceptance Meditation' can help break down the barrier of shame, encouraging a mindset of acceptance and self-love. By actively engaging with these tools, we start the process of identifying where shame is influencing our lives and start dismantling it.

It is also important to note that shame tends to thrive in secrecy, gaining strength when kept hidden and unaddressed. Opening up and being honest about our feelings with someone we can trust and sharing our truth can become a powerful way to break through the barrier of shame. By breaking the silence, we lessen the grip of shame, creating space for understanding, empathy and support, freeing ourselves to move forward without the burdens that may otherwise hold us back.

For Alex's journey, the emphasis was on connecting with his authentic self and letting go of the distorted reality he once believed to be true. For him to see his real self, a wonderful intelligent person who is worthy of being loved by himself and others, it required working through genuine self-acceptance. Initially, this shift was uncomfortable for Alex, who was used to hiding behind a protective layer. Stepping into authenticity made him feel exposed and vulnerable, heightening his anxiety. Yet, through consistent practice of self-compassion and acceptance, and giving himself time to adjust, it gradually became easier. Alex took small but courageous steps, like engaging in social settings and pursuing hobbies aligned with his genuine interests, rather than choosing what felt easier to navigate with his feelings of insecurity and shame.

Recognising and addressing deep-seated emotions are crucial steps in overcoming the barriers that stem from past experiences. It requires empathy, self-reflection and sometimes professional support to navigate the journey towards healing and building a healthier self-worth. Alex's story highlights the resilience needed to confront and move beyond the shadows of the past towards a more empowered and confident self. It's important to understand that feelings of shame and insecurity are complex and can often be deeply rooted in past traumas.

Super Power Booster Pack

The next step was to assist Alex in navigating social situations with confidence, so we introduced the concept of a 'Super Power Booster Pack'. This imaginary backpack was filled with his values and strengths. Alex could mentally strap on this pack whenever he ventured out, reminding himself of the value he brought to any interaction. The more he focused on acknowledging and nurturing what made him unique, the more he could see the value within himself. He started to feel confident to venture out and try new things, to slowly make connections with new people. Focusing on new hobbies created opportunities for connections with like-minded people. With every positive interaction, Alex's confidence grew, and he bravely started to show the world his true self.

Super Power Booster Pack

Alex's Super Power Booster Pack consisted of two key components: his personal values and his strengths. Building your own Super Power Booster Pack is a simple process. Let's begin by understanding what values are and how you can identify your own.

The Value of Values

Our values are the core principles that guide our life, influencing how we live, love and work. Values are an internal part of our BE-ing. They reflect what is important to us, what we stand for and what we prioritise. They influence our behaviours, decisions and interactions with others and serve as our code of conduct, guiding us through life's choices and challenges.

They act a bit like a compass, helping us navigate our path and to determine whether our actions are in alignment with our true self. When we honour our values, we experience a sense of clarity and stability. However, when we neglect or compromise our values, we may feel a sense of disconnection and dissatisfaction.

Embracing our values strengthens our inner sense of worth and fosters a deep connection to our authentic self. There is a wide range of values, for example honesty, integrity, compassion, financial security, health/fitness, nature, accomplishment, dependability, loyalty, beauty, bravery, love, connection/relationships, learning, survival, self-preservation, security, adventure, family, work, success, calm, freedom, creativity, gratitude and leadership.

Honouring our values is not about sticking to a set of rules; it's about honouring our inner worthiness and staying true to who we are at our core. When we have that sense of stability within ourselves, in times of uncertainty or when faced with important decisions, we can rely on our values as a guide, helping us navigate the complexities of life with clarity and integrity. By understanding our values and honouring them in our choices, we can then align our actions to match what is truly important to us and create positive outcomes.

When we don't live by our values or are unaware of them, we are more likely to fall into bad habits and regress into patterns of behaviour that do not serve us well. This can lead to feelings of being lost, unsatisfied and like we are settling for a life that does not truly fulfil us.

As we saw in Alex's case in the previous chapter, he struggled with seeking self-worth through people-pleasing behaviours for many years. When we explored his values, Alex discovered that besides 'being a good person', meaningful relationships and honesty were among his other core values. However, due to years of bullying, he developed unhealthy habits to maintain some form of connection with others. Spending excessive time online anonymously and accepting work requests he didn't truly want were his attempts to seek validation. Yet, these actions left him feeling drained and unfulfilled because they didn't align with his values, leading to a sense of disconnection from what truly mattered to him and a decline in self-worth.

Once Alex recognised this pattern and understood its roots, we worked on finding actions that better aligned with his core values of meaningful relationships and honesty. For Alex, this meant first examining his behaviour and being honest with himself, so he could authentically engage with others and cre-

ate genuine connections. He realised that having meaningful relationships with honest people required him to be honest with himself first and show up as his authentic self. By focusing on his values, Alex gained clarity on where to invest his energy and how to maintain integrity within himself, guiding him in his interactions with others. This process also encouraged him to seek connections in new, healthier ways, moving away from old patterns that no longer served him.

How to Identify Your Values

Identifying your values can sometimes be challenging, especially when influenced by external factors or societal norms, often leading us to operate on autopilot, without truly understanding what drives us. If you're unsure about your values or feel like it's time for a refresh, let's have a look together. Grab a piece of paper, a pen, or better yet, a notebook to jot down your thoughts for future reflection. Let's begin by answering the following questions:

First, let's reflect for a minute on your happiest memory.

- Can you briefly describe this memory?
- What were you doing during that moment?
- Why do you think that experience brought you immense joy?

Now let's dig a bit deeper and take your time writing down your answers in a few sentences:

Recall a moment in your life when you felt most proud of yourself.

- What specific action or achievement are you proud of?
- Why do you believe this moment fills you with pride?

For the next few questions, you can jot down brief answers. We're almost there!

- Can you write down what holds the greatest importance in your life?
- Can you remember instances when you felt truly good about yourself?

Think about a role model whom you deeply admire.

- What qualities in their personalities and/or daily practices do you find most inspiring?

And lastly,

- Can you name two aspects of the world around you that you wish to see improved?

Reflecting on your answers, do you think you can list six of your values? Notice any recurring themes in your answers that point to the same value. This repetition may indicate that this value holds significant importance to you. If you need some guidance, here's a list of examples to consider. Keep in mind that these are just examples, as there's a wide range of values.

- Honesty
- Integrity
- Compassion
- Financial security
- Health
- Fitness
- Nature
- Accomplishment
- Dependability
- Loyalty
- Bravery
- Love
- Connection
- Meaningful relationships
- Learning
- Survival
- Security
- Adventure
- Family
- Work
- Success
- Calm
- Freedom
- Creativity
- Gratitude
- Leadership

Once you've pinpointed your six personal values, take a moment to validate them. Reflect on whether these values truly resonate with you and make you feel good about yourself. Can you genuinely stand behind them with conviction? If so, that's fantastic! Now, it's time to actively integrate these values into your daily choices. Consider placing them somewhere visible, like on the fridge, by your bedside or on your phone screen, to serve as daily reminders of what truly matters to you. By keeping your focus on these values in your everyday actions, relationships and routines, you'll begin to notice a shift in your life. Things will start to fall into place, and you'll experience a sense of stability and contentment within yourself.

Now, let's delve into Drew's story.

Drew

Drew is a hard-working man with a young family. He takes immense pride in providing for his loved ones and running his own business. However, as his business demands increased, Drew found himself spending less and less time with his family. Despite waking up before dawn to squeeze in extra work hours, Drew still finds himself struggling to strike a balance between his professional responsibilities and spending quality time with his family. This imbalance has put a strain on his relationship, leaving his wife feeling overwhelmed and unsupported. She longs for his support and companionship, but Drew's busy schedule leaves him exhausted and unavailable, further increasing the tension between them.

During our session, Drew opened up about feeling disconnected from the fulfilling life he once enjoyed. He reminisced about a time when he felt incredibly fortunate and content with his work, family and friendships. However, a noticeable shift had occurred recently. As his schedule became more demanding, he found himself struggling to maintain the balance he once had. Arguments with his wife became more frequent, and finding moments of quality time amidst their busy lives seemed like an impossible task. Unsure of how to address these challenges, Drew buried himself in his work, where he still felt a sense of purpose. Unfortunately, this only intensified the sense of disconnection he experienced at home, leaving him feeling drained and depleted. Drew longed for the meaningful connections he once shared with his family and friends, realising how much he missed the bond with his wife and the camaraderie with his friends.

Together, Drew and I explored his values and identified six personal values that resonated deeply with him: meaningful relationships, family, dependability, connection, adventure and freedom. Through this process, Drew gained clarity on the areas of his life where he had deviated from his values, leading to feelings of dissatisfaction and disconnection. He saw clearly where he had veered off course from his authentic self. The realisation struck hard – he expressed that he felt his family, whom he loved deeply, couldn't depend on him as they deserved, and he felt disappointed with himself for not being the present and engaged father he aimed to be. Additionally, he sensed a growing distance between himself and his wife, causing him great distress. The lack of adventure and freedom, which used to be essential parts of their family life, made Drew long for the happiness and excitement they experienced during camping trips and weekend getaways. The lost connections with his friends also weighed heavily on him.

With this newfound clarity, Drew understood how living out of alignment with his values had eroded his sense of self-worth, casting a shadow over his happiness and fulfilment. Drew was eager to initiate change and realised he couldn't do this alone. Together with his wife, they sat down and crafted a plan to reclaim a sense of balance and connection in their lives.

Acknowledging his priorities, Drew opted to hire an assistant for his business, giving himself more time to spend with his family, including a three-day weekend for quality time. The family resumed their monthly camping trips, creating beautiful memories full of adventure. Drew also made an effort to prioritise his social life, attending a weekly sporting class with friends and establishing a dedicated date night with his wife. As a result, his relationship with his wife blossomed, and he found immense joy in being fully present with his children. With his life in harmony once more, Drew rediscovered fulfilment in his roles as an individual, father, partner and friend. These positive changes even extended to his business, giving him a newfound sense of inspiration.

Understanding and living in alignment with your values not only reinforces your sense of worthiness but also nurtures deeper connections with yourself and others, thereby filling your Wellbeing Cup. On the other hand, living out of alignment with your values can lead to feelings of instability and disconnection, ultimately draining your cup, as experienced by both Alex and Drew.

Now that you have a deeper understanding of the value of values and have identified your six personal ones for your Super Power Booster Pack, let's shift our focus to your strengths.

Super Power Booster Pack

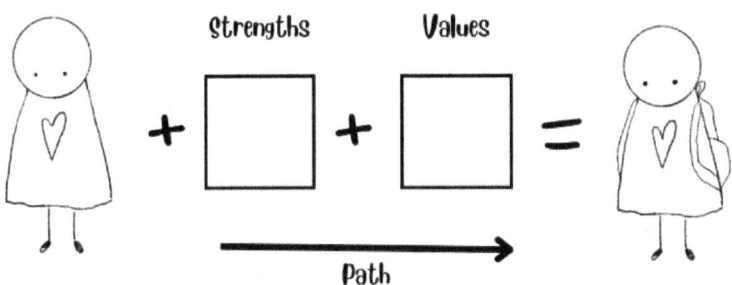
Path

Strengths

Your strengths are your natural abilities, the things you are effortlessly good at and often overlook, assuming everyone shares similar talents. However, each of us has a special blend of strengths that makes us unique. It's often what others notice about you, but you are unaware of. Your strengths are invaluable assets that play an important role in your personal growth and pursuit of social freedom. When you recognise and actively use your strengths, you can integrate them into your daily life, allowing you to navigate challenges with greater ease and authenticity and create more meaningful connections with others.

Now, imagine reframing your strengths not merely as attributes but as superpowers – powerful assets you can pack into your SPB Pack to thrive in social situations, or whenever you need an empowering boost. By shifting your perspective in this way, you see yourself as a powerful force capable of propelling you forward into action.

You might already have a clear understanding of your strengths, or perhaps you're still figuring them out. If you're in the second group, here's some guidance on identifying your unique strengths. It involves a process of self-reflection and assessment.

Here are some examples, keep in mind that everyone has a unique mix of strengths.

- Creativity
- Leadership
- Problem-solving skills
- Resilience
- Adaptability
- Communication skills
- Empathy
- Teamwork
- Organisation
- Perseverance
- Patience
- Flexibility
- Integrity
- Initiative
- Attention to detail
- Open-mindedness
- Confidence

Here are some steps you can take to identify your strengths:

- Reflect on your experiences, achievements and activities that come naturally to you. Recall moments when you felt confident and accomplished, and consider the skills and qualities that contributed to those successes. Think about how you can leverage these strengths in the future.
- Think back on past life experiences that were challenging for you and consider how you coped with

those difficulties. Were there moments where you relied on your inner strengths to overcome obstacles?
- Seek feedback from people whose opinions you trust, such as friends, family, colleagues or mentors. They can provide valuable insights into your strengths based on their observations of you.
- Engage in new activities and challenges to explore areas where you excel and find enjoyment. Pay attention to tasks that come naturally to you and those that bring you a sense of fulfilment.
- Keep a Strengths Journal. Document instances when you feel strong and capable in a journal. Note down activities or tasks that energise you and contribute to your sense of fulfilment.
- Look for patterns or themes in your strengths across different areas of your life, such as work, relationships and hobbies. Identifying recurring strengths can offer valuable insights into your unique abilities.

By taking these steps, you'll gain a deeper understanding of your strengths and how to use them to support yourself in all areas of life. When you combine your strengths with your values, you become unstoppable on your path. This sense of empowerment transforms feelings of insecurity into feelings of worthiness, empowering us to take decisive action.

In the upcoming chapter, we explore how to take decisive action as we delve into the Action Stage, where we create meaningful shifts and bring our aspirations to life.

Recall our exploration of the emotion Insecure in Part 1, where we applied the SFUC method. Now, let's revisit this section armed with our understanding of the Empowerment Stage.

SFUC Method for Insecure:

Stop: Take a deep breath.

Feel: Take a moment to ask yourself, "How am I feeling?"

Example: I am unsure about the situation, so I don't feel comfortable to say anything, as I don't want to look odd. Everyone is probably looking at me, which is making me feel nervous.

Understand: Why am I feeling like this?

Feelings of insecurity and unworthiness can significantly impact how I handle situations and interact with people in my life. These feelings often lead to self-doubt and a lack of self-confidence. This can make it challenging to express myself authentically and make decisions confidently. These feelings can create a self-fulfilling cycle where I perceive myself as inadequate, which then influences how I engage with others and the world around me.

Connect: Try answering the following questions:

1. What could be the root cause of these feelings I have about being unworthy or not good enough?

2. Am I conscious of the fact that I am a unique individual with my own strengths and values?
3. Am I using my unique strengths to propel myself forward in life?
4. Do I have a clear understanding of my values, and am I fully committed to standing behind them without any doubt?
5. Am I actively seeking opportunities to act on matters that align with my values?
6. Am I playing small and limiting my potential? What is driving this behaviour?

The Action Stage

Welcome to the Action Stage, a stage where we courageously venture beyond our comfort zones and embrace the future with a sense of empowerment. Here, we operate from a foundation of alignment and integrity, driven by purposeful action. Guided by our values and fuelled by our strengths, we move forward optimistically, infused with self-compassion, ready to create meaningful shifts and bring our aspirations to life. This stage represents a period of active engagement, where every step forward is purposeful and deliberate.

In this stage, as with previous ones, certain emotions may surface. Feelings of overwhelm may arise, making it seem nearly impossible to move forward. However, with a deeper understanding of this emotion and effective strategies in place, we can find ways to manage it, regain control and restore balance to our lives. This helps us to take on whatever challenges lie ahead, with integrity and intentional action.

Feeling Overwhelmed

Feeling overwhelmed is a common emotion, particularly when we're faced with the challenge of taking action. It's that feeling of being mentally or emotionally flooded, where the weight of tasks, responsibilities and stimuli becomes almost suffocating, making it difficult to cope effectively. This sensation can manifest as stress, anxiety or a sense of being unable to manage or prioritise tasks. The feeling of being overwhelmed often arises when there's a mismatch between the demands placed on us and our perceived ability to handle those demands.

The sensation of being overwhelmed is like being caught in a whirlwind of emotions and thoughts, where everything seems to happen all at once, and life moves faster than we can process. It's a state of paralysis and confusion, where productivity and our ability to focus take a back seat to the sudden flood of current circumstances. Life can feel incredibly stressful in those moments, and the instinct to hide away can be strong. However, it's crucial to pause, take a deep breath and regroup. Implementing strategies like the BE SMART acronym from 'The Awareness Stage' can help guide us back to the present moment and calm our nervous system.

Taking a break and engaging in activities that promote relaxation and wellbeing, such as exercise, meditation or spending time outdoors, can ground us and improve our focus. If engaging in those activities isn't possible, we can still manage the feeling of being overwhelmed by practising mindfulness techniques on the spot. Simple practices like deep breathing can quickly reduce stress levels and improve our capacity to make clear, thoughtful decisions about our next steps. This offers a way to regain our composure and feel more in control, even during challenging circumstances.

Once we regain our clarity and focus, we can approach the overwhelming situation with a more strategic mindset. We can start by breaking down the tasks at hand into smaller, manageable steps, focusing on completing one step at a time, to prevent feeling overwhelmed again. By adopting a realistic mindset about what we can accomplish, we allow ourselves to be compassionate towards ourselves and create a plan of action that aligns with our current capacity. This plan should include actionable steps that move us closer to the desired outcome, helping us to regain a sense of control over the situation.

Additionally, setting clear boundaries with both ourselves and others is important. Learning to say no to additional demands and commitments that may contribute to us feeling overwhelmed, and establishing boundaries to protect our time and energy are essential practices for maintaining a sense of control. By practising self-compassion and prioritising these strategies, we can gift ourselves the ability to overcome overwhelming situations.

Lastly, it's essential to believe in ourselves and our ability to overcome feelings of being overwhelmed. Reconnecting with our sense of self-worth empowers us to recognise our strength and capability to make changes and move forward.

Here's a recap of the strategies to help you cope when you're feeling overwhelmed:

- Pause, take a deep breath and regroup.
- Implement strategies like the BE SMART acronym to guide yourself back to the present moment.
- Practice mindfulness techniques such as deep breathing to reduce stress and improve decision-making.
- Once you regain focus and clarity, think about how you can strategically approach the task/situation at hand.
- Break tasks into smaller, manageable steps.
- Focus on completing them one step at a time.
- Maintain realistic expectations about what can be accomplished, you are only human after all!
- Set clear boundaries to safeguard your time and energy.
- Believe in yourself and trust in your ability to manage when you are feeling overwhelmed.

Working in Alignment with Our Values

Working in alignment with our values can be a powerful tool for reducing feelings of being overwhelmed and regaining a sense of control in our lives.

Take Drew for example, whom we met in the Empowerment chapter. Drew found himself struggling to keep his life balanced, feeling overwhelmed by the challenges he faced. However, it wasn't until he realised that he wasn't living in line with his true values that he began to see a way forward. By identifying his values and making choices that aligned with them, Drew experienced a positive change. He and his wife developed a plan to reclaim balance in their lives, which allowed Drew to take decisive action and regain control.

Now, let's explore how you can align your actions with your values to create positive change in your life. Take a moment to revisit your values. If you've written them down before, grab your notebook or piece of paper where you've documented them. If not, take a moment to head back to the Empowerment chapter and write down your values.

Reflecting on your values, consider the actions necessary to align your life more closely with them. For example, if, like Drew, one of your values is 'Dependability', think about what actions you can take to embody it more fully. Next, ask yourself the following three questions to gain clarity and direction:

1. What kind of action do I need to take to live by my values?
2. What actions are leading me further away from embodying my values?
3. What actions can bring me closer to living in alignment with my values?

For Drew, this might involve:

1. Prioritising family time and reducing his workload.
2. Spending more hours at work and being unavailable on weekends for his family
3. Hiring an assistant to help with the workload and spending quality time with his family on weekends

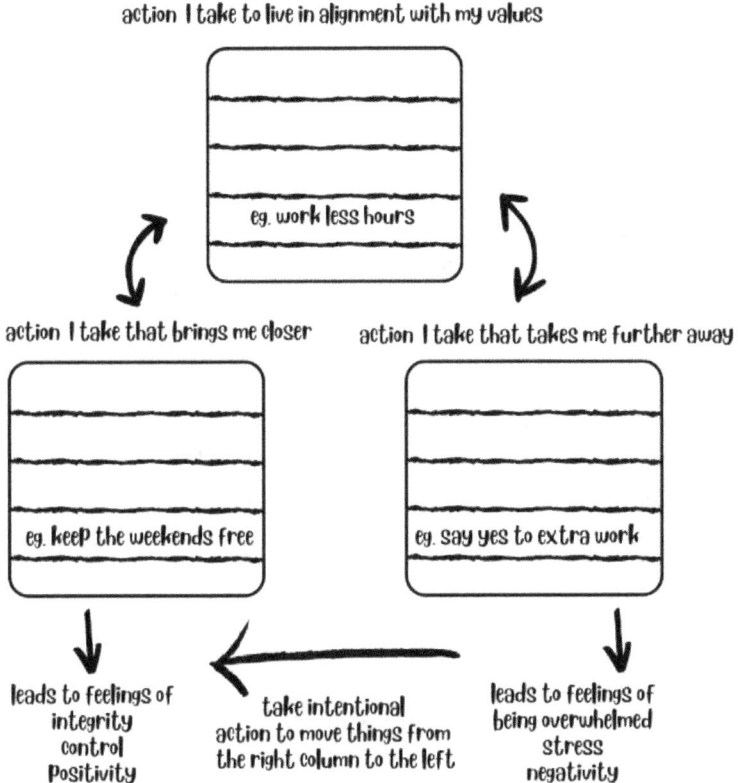

Choosing actions that align with our values not only fosters positive emotions but also reduces feelings of being overwhelmed, as we become more accustomed to living in alignment. On the other hand, living out of alignment with our values leads us down the opposite path, as the gap between our actions and our values becomes bigger, as illustrated in the graph below.

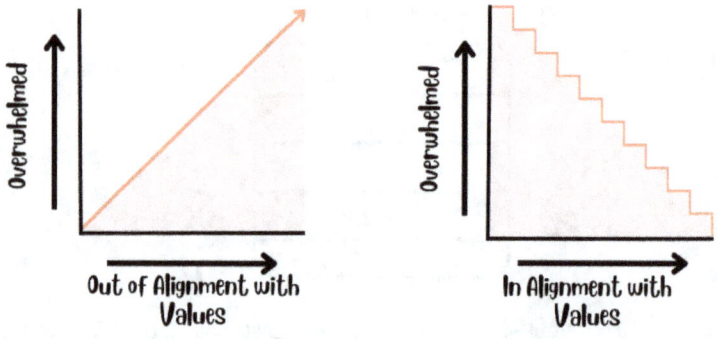

Now that we have a deeper understanding of the emotion of feeling overwhelmed, let's explore how we can create meaningful shifts and bring our aspirations to life. The Action Stage represents a period of active engagement, where every step forward is purposeful and deliberate, placing the focus on intentional action.

Moving Forward with Intentional Action and Integrity

When we take action that brings us closer to our values, we experience a sense of alignment, integrity, positivity and control. On the other hand, when our actions lead us further from our values, we tend to feel more overwhelmed, stressed and negative. That is why it can be valuable to do regular check-ins with ourselves, helping us stay honest about our actions and behaviours. It's common to revert to old habits without even realising it, but by being aware of what might draw us back, we can recognise these patterns as they emerge. This awareness provides us with the opportunity to redirect ourselves from our old ways to a new, aligned version of ourselves.

For example, Drew might be accustomed to saying yes to more work, as his value of being dependable spills over into his professional life. However, in doing so, he might unintentionally neglect his promise to his family, thereby straying from his commitment to live by his values. Recognising these patterns helps him practise intentional action with integrity.

Intentional Action

Intentional action involves taking steps that are in alignment with our true selves, guided by self-compassion for what truly matters to us and an understanding of our current capacity. It requires bravery to stretch ourselves within our capabilities and rely on our resilience and strengths to overcome obstacles. It's about moving forward with purpose and authenticity, making choices that honour our values and lead us towards the future we desire. In short, it requires consistency between our intentions, values and actions.

It may come as a surprise that this isn't a time for DO-ing; quite the contrary, more than ever, it's a time for BE-ing. It's about reconnecting with ourselves and moving forward authentically, guided by our inner compass. It's about tuning in and recognising that the answers we seek reside within us. When we align with our true selves, we maintain focus on what truly matters, avoiding distractions and comparisons with others and thereby embracing intentional action and honouring our integrity.

Integrity

Integrity, defined as the quality of moral consistency and truthfulness with oneself and others, plays a crucial role in intentional action. It involves living authentically, with our values and beliefs reflected in our outwards behaviour. When we act with integrity, we uphold our commitments and take responsibility for our actions. The word integrity comes from the Latin integritas and interestingly means wholeness.

Joanne's story demonstrates the intersection of intentional action and integrity.

Joanne

Joanne, a lovely lady, found herself struggling mentally following a health scare that turned her world upside down. The diagnosis of severe health issues left her feeling overwhelmed and unsure of where to start. Homebound and unable to work, her doctor prescribed a complete overhaul of her diet, including dietary restrictions. Additionally, she was advised to join a local gym, a task that felt daunting for someone who had never done this before.

From the start, Joanne struggled with the idea of making such significant changes. She felt completely overwhelmed by the thought of altering her lifestyle and was unsure of her ability to stick to the doctor's recommendations. Amidst her feelings of anxiety about her new circumstances and a paralysing sense of being overwhelmed, Joanne found herself feeling stuck and unable to move forward. She recognised the need for change but felt unable to take the necessary steps.

In approaching Joanne's situation, the focus was on meeting her where she was emotionally. Recognising that pushing her to take immediate action would only heighten her feelings of being overwhelmed, we began with the Acceptance Stage. Together, we acknowledged the reality of her circumstances, fostering self-compassion for the changes she was experiencing and helping her come to terms with the adjustments ahead.

Through open dialogue and gentle encouragement, Joanne began to slowly shift her perspective and recognise her role in her own health journey and the work it would take for her to get better. With a newfound sense of accountability, Joanne started to take ownership of her health and wellbeing. We worked on incorporating daily practices to manage her anxiety, cultivate her self-worth and build resilience, allowing her to overcome her fears and manage her new routine. Through this process, Joanne began to understand that it was not up to her doctor, her personal trainer or her family to push her to take her health seriously, rather, the power to change lay within herself.

As we transitioned into the Empowerment Stage, we delved into Joanne's values. Spending time in nature and with family emerged as important ones. She loved going for walks with her dog and her family in the forest, and as Joanne gained clarity on her values, she also understood why being healthy would be important to her. Connecting her desire to spend time with her dog and her family in nature, to her commitment to becoming healthy, made it easier to stick to her prescribed diet and gave her determination. She also noticed which actions brought her closer to, or further away from her health goals. With a personalised plan outlining small, manageable steps, Joanne started taking intentional action.

However, sticking to her plan wasn't always easy for Joanne. There were days when the thought of going to the gym was the last thing she wanted and moments at parties where sticking to her dietary restrictions felt like a real challenge. The pressure to indulge, to avoid seeming rude, was sometimes overwhelming. However, the consequences of deviating from her plan were severe. On every occasion, she fell ill, sometimes enduring setbacks in her health that lasted for weeks.

These experiences served as a wake-up call, reminding her of the importance of prioritising her health above all else. Joanne realised that in her efforts to please others, she had inadvertently compromised her wellbeing. Over time, she established a routine and strictly stuck to her commitments. As she began to feel the positive effects of her choices, she grew increasingly reluctant to compromise her health. By taking responsibility for her actions and consistently living with integrity, Joanne kept taking actions to turn her health around.

Living with integrity means staying true to ourselves, even when it's difficult. It involves making decisions based on our own values, rather than external pressures or societal expectations. People with integrity uphold their commitments and take responsibility for their actions. Furthermore, practising integrity requires mindfulness and awareness. It involves regularly examining our thoughts, beliefs and actions, to ensure they are still aligning with our values. It also entails taking responsibility for our mistakes, learning from them and taking action to move forward with new intent.

As you saw with Joanne, the feeling of being overwhelmed by her circumstances was a significant barrier to progress and taking action. Once she recognised that her overwhelm stemmed from a mismatch between the demands placed on her and her perceived ability to manage them, she could begin to work on implementing changes by focusing on gradually shifting her perception. We did this by using tools and practices from various stages leading up to the Action Stage. As Joanne became used to using these tools and gained confidence in her ability to handle demands, we moved towards taking intentional action, and to prevent overwhelm, we broke down the steps into manageable tasks. This allowed Joanne to feel more in control and witness positive changes at a pace that suited her current circumstances.

Intentional action has the remarkable power to create meaningful shifts in your life, far beyond surface adjustments, setting the course towards the life you truly long for. Therefore, to conclude this chapter, I'll leave you with three questions that are designed to prompt reflection and inspire intentional action:

1. What immediate changes would you make to improve your life if everything stayed the same as it is now?
2. Envision your future self. Describe the kind of person you aspire to become. What steps can you take now to align with this vision?
3. If you could create your dream life without any limitations, what would it look like? Dream big and visualise your ideal scenario. Then, trace back in time and consider what steps you can take in the near future to start moving towards this dream life.

Question One prompts you to create your short-term action plan, consisting of small steps that you can begin implementing immediately. While these steps may appear minor, they have the potential to make a big difference over time.

Question Two prompts you to reflect on your mid-term action plan and relates to the Alignment Exercise we worked on in this chapter. Consider what you are currently doing that may hinder your progress and what actions bring you closer. By identifying areas for improvement, you can make significant changes. Don't be surprised if big shifts suddenly start to happen!

Question Three encourages you to consider your long-term action plan, consisting of gradual steps that you can work on over time. These actions should complement and align with your short and mid-term plans, contributing to your overarching vision. By breaking down your long-term objectives into manageable steps and integrating them with your short-term plans, you can maintain momentum and progress steadily towards your desired outcomes.

Remember, consistency and perseverance are key as you chip away at your action plan, knowing that each small step contributes to your larger vision for the future. In the next chapter, we explore the Achievement Stage, where intentional action merges with our vitality, propelling us towards remarkable accomplishments.

Recall our exploration of the emotion of feeling Overwhelmed in Part 1, where we applied the SFUC method. Now, let's revisit this section armed with our understanding of the Action Stage.

SFUC Method When Feeling Overwhelmed:

Stop: Take a deep breath.

Feel: Take a moment to ask yourself, "How am I feeling?"

Example: It feels like everything is happening all at once, it's becoming quite overwhelming, and I'm recognising the need to take a step back as I seem unable to manage or prioritise tasks.

Understand: Why am I feeling like this?

I'm feeling overwhelmed because life is moving at a pace that's challenging for my mind and nervous system to keep up with. This feeling can arise when there's a mismatch between the demands placed on me and my perceived ability to handle those demands. As a result, I may feel paralysed and find it difficult to take action.

Connect: Try answering the following questions:

1. Can I think of strategies I can use to slow things down, to bring a sense of calm into my life?
2. What is most important right now?
3. How can I channel my energy and time into the most important tasks and objectives?
4. Can I think of a way to deconstruct complex issues into smaller, manageable parts?
5. How can I develop a step-by-step plan to move forward on these smaller parts, thereby creating a sense of accomplishment and soothing my nervous system?

The Achievement Stage

Welcome to the Achievement Stage, where our cup is nearly full, brimming with energy and readiness to focus on the task at hand. This stage marks an important moment in our journey, where intentional action merges with our vitality, propelling us towards remarkable accomplishments. In this phase, we establish sustainable wellbeing practices to maintain our energy levels and amplify our productivity. By nurturing ourselves through these practices, we ensure that our cup remains replenished, empowering us to pursue our deepest desires and aspirations.

These practices not only energise us but also provide us with the ability to appreciate our achievements. As we reflect on our accomplishments, we cultivate a deep sense of gratitude for the journey we've undertaken. Each success becomes a source of inspiration, fuelling us with renewed energy to pursue even greater accomplishments. As we witness the results of our efforts, we come to understand that the life we desire is within our reach. Driven by purpose and connected to our inner wisdom, we are propelled forward with a sense of determination and clarity.

In the Achievement Stage, we enter a state of flow where our actions seamlessly align with our aspirations. We become a source of creativity and innovation, drawing from an infinite well of inspiration. With every accomplishment, we actualise our potential and make meaningful contributions to the world. Embracing this stage, we acknowledge the power of BE-ing, realising that we can perform at our best when we are aligned with our authentic selves.

Running on Empty

In this chapter, we explore the concept of replenishing our energy reserves to fuel our achievements. We delve into how our accomplishments can, in turn, recharge us with renewed energy. When we're attuned to our mind, body and soul, we become better listeners to our own needs. We understand that just as we can't pour from an empty cup, we need to fill ourselves up first to be able to succeed. Recognising when we're running low on energy is crucial – it's not a sign of failure but rather an indication that we may need to re-evaluate our approach. It's a time for reflection and recalibration, not just pushing through blindly.

When we're depleted, it's a signal to pause, reset and refill to prevent burnout. We must harness our energy and intentionality shift our behaviour to ensure that our wellbeing remains intact. This becomes our priority, as it is the key to unlocking the door to regaining energy. Energy is crucial for achievement, as it counteracts feelings of being drained. Feeling drained is a gradual depletion and eventual deprivation of essential resources necessary for existence, stemming from prolonged exposure to stressors.

Stressors that drain our energy can include:

- Insufficient sleep or rest.
- Pushing ourselves too hard physically, mentally or emotionally without adequate breaks.

- Engaging in tasks or activities that don't align with our values or passions.
- Inadequate nutrition and hydration.
- Failing to set boundaries with others or ourselves.
- Work-related pressures such as deadlines, workload and job insecurity.
- Relationship challenges with family members, friends or romantic partners.
- Financial concerns about money, debt or financial instability.
- Dealing with illness, chronic pain or caring for sick family members.
- Major life changes such as moving, starting a new job or going through a divorce.
- Social pressures and expectations from society, cultural norms or social media.
- Personal challenges such as struggles with self-esteem, perfectionism or unresolved past traumas.

Feeling drained is like slowly running out of fuel. It's a state of emptiness where our mind, body and soul yearn for renewal, yet we struggle to find the energy to keep going. As reserves dwindle, the need to replenish becomes apparent; our cup is nearing empty, signalling the time for a refill.

To replenish our energy, we can adopt sustainable wellbeing practices that keep us consistently topped up, preventing us from reaching such depleted states. Having reserves to draw from becomes extremely important in times of need. Ideally, during periods of stability, we aim to fill our cup to the brim, allowing us to tap into the overflow during challenging times. Let's look at some strategies we can use to fill our cup, but first let me introduce Britt.

Britt

Meet Britt, a single mother of two and a dedicated entrepreneur, who found herself on the brink of burnout. Juggling the responsibilities of parenting and managing her business, she was exhausted, barely able to make it through each day. Britt's schedule was packed, often stretching into late hours, as she tackled unfinished tasks after her children had gone to bed. When I enquired about her relaxation habits, she mentioned attending a weekly yoga class and occasionally catching snippets of a movie while folding laundry or chatting with her mom during her commute after dropping her kids off at school. It was clear that Britt was constantly on the move, juggling her numerous responsibilities with very little time for herself.

During our sessions, we delved into the concepts of self-care, protecting your energy and the significance of the three Wellbeing Cups, which I'll discuss later in this chapter. I stressed the importance of prioritising self-care while she still has control over her health, emphasising that neglecting her wellbeing would only lead to further decline. Together, we explored the effects of guilt associated with taking time for one-

self and the critical importance of recognising that one cannot pour from an empty cup. Burnout is simply the result of an empty cup, benefiting no one.

We pinpointed the areas of imbalance in Britt's life, identifying the energy drains stemming from her dual roles as caregiver and business owner. It became evident that attempting to operate at an achievement level with an empty tank was unsustainable. Therefore, we focused on tuning into the body's wisdom, paying attention to its cues and signals. Sometimes, it was as simple as recognising the need to take a break to use the restroom, eat regular meals or prioritise sleep at a reasonable hour, even when there were many tasks demanding attention.

Our Inner Wisdom

Filling our cup is closely linked to our connection with our inner wisdom, which encompasses the harmony between our mind, body and soul. When this connection is balanced, we experience clarity of thought, make sound decisions and navigate our emotions effectively.

Understanding and regulating our emotions is vital for our social freedom and overall wellbeing. In a state of alignment, our mind, body and soul can communicate seamlessly, allowing us to introspect and gauge our feelings about specific life situations. We can tune in and listen to their responses, discern whether acting on a particular emotion is beneficial and determine the way to move forward. This synergy empowers us to make informed decisions that honour our holistic wellbeing, integrating the insights from all aspects of our BE-ing.

We can harness this wisdom to replenish our energy for focused achievement, merging our vitality with intentional action. We do this by employing the concept of the three Wellbeing Cups.

These cups serve as tools to help us identify what drains our energy and what re-energises us. Despite our best efforts to maintain balance, life's complexities may sometimes cause our cups to run low. By adopting a proactive approach, we work on prevention to ensure we have reserves available. When we sense our energy dwindling, we take immediate action to refill them. We become the fierce protectors of our Wellbeing Cups.

The Three Wellbeing Cups

The Mind, Body and Soul Cups

As we observed with Britt, navigating life with an empty cup can be incredibly challenging. The constant juggling act between family and business responsibilities left her feeling drained and disconnected from her own needs. Recognising that she was dangerously close to burnout, she knew something had to change. Despite her reluctance to make adjustments, she could no longer ignore the toll it was taking on her.

Exhausted and overwhelmed, Britt found herself resenting the never ending to-do list and struggling to keep up. She experienced a sense of isolation from her friends, frustration with her children and disappointment in herself for falling short of meeting all expectations. Yet, the idea of prioritising herself seemed extremely daunting amidst the chaos of daily life. It somehow seemed easier to continue as she always had.

Throughout our sessions, we delved into the concept of accountability and its direct link to replenishing our Wellbeing Cups. I emphasised that without taking responsibility for actively prioritising her wellbeing, especially when it feels overwhelming, her cups will remain empty. For Britt, this meant first acknowledging her energy gaps, understanding the significance of setting clear boundaries, recognising energy vampires and understanding the draining impact of the constant DO-ing state.

The concept of the three Wellbeing Cups is a framework designed to help you identify, prioritise and manage what energises and what drains you. These cups represent different aspects of wellbeing, each contributing to your overall health and vitality. Here's a breakdown of the three Wellbeing Cups:

The Mind Cup is all about nurturing your mental and emotional wellbeing, focusing on cultivating a healthy mindset and emotional balance. Filling the Mind Cup may include practices such as mindfulness meditation, positive mental stimulation, engaging in hobbies or activities that bring joy, seeking therapy or counselling when needed and cultivating positive thought patterns.

The Body Cup represents your physical wellbeing, including aspects such as nutrition, exercise, sleep and overall physical health. Filling the Body Cup involves listening to what our body needs and activities that nourish the body, for example, eating balanced meals, engaging in regular physical activity and getting sufficient sleep.

The Soul Cup represents our wisdom and intuition, including practices that give us a sense of purpose, connection and fulfilment. Filling the Soul Cup may include practices that connect us to our authentic selves, living in alignment with our values and creating a purposeful life.

Before Britt could fully commit to her three Wellbeing Cups practice, we focused on a blend of accountability techniques, including boundary-setting methods and mindfulness practices for energy allocation. As she delved deeper into these practices, she began to grasp that being in a state of BE-ing was more than just a state of existence – it was about being present, stable and at peace with oneself. With this newfound awareness and the tools provided, she learnt to consciously redirect her energy and close the gaps that were draining her vitality.

To initiate more change, we carved out daily pockets of time for Britt to embrace silence and engage in nurturing activities like reading, meditation and nature walks. Initially, Britt found it challenging to shift away from the constant busyness that provided her with a dopamine fix. Transitioning to a focus on slow self-care and being present felt unfamiliar and even boring to her. She experienced restlessness and extreme fatigue, as her body and mind were not accustomed to pausing.

Feelings of unworthiness surfaced because she strongly tied her self-worth to her achievements. To address this, we focused on shifting her mindset towards feelings of empowerment derived from taking care of herself. By emphasising the importance of self-care, Britt realised that prioritising her wellbeing enabled her to better support those who depended on her. With each step forward, Britt became increasingly focused on protecting her energy. By integrating the principles of the three Wellbeing Cups into her routine, she began to notice positive changes.

Refilling Your Cups

Now, let's explore what replenishes your cups. Could you list three activities that nourish each of your Wellbeing Cups? Additionally, identify three factors that deplete them. Below are some examples to guide you.

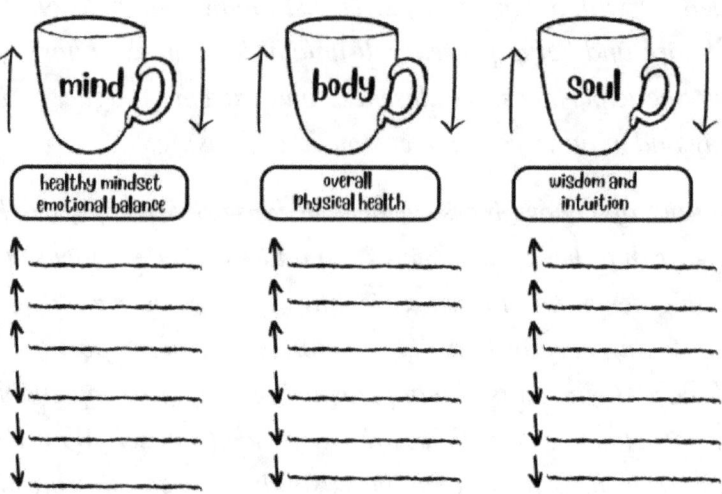

Mind Cup Fillers:

1. Reading inspirational books or articles.
2. Engaging in stimulating conversations with friends.

3. Practising mindfulness meditation.

Mind Cup Drainers:

1. Overthinking and excessive worrying.
2. Exposure to prolonged screen time.
3. Engaging with energy vampires.

Body Cup Fillers:

1. Regular exercise.
2. Eating nourishing and balanced meals.
3. Getting enough restorative sleep.

Body Cup Drainers:

1. Poor dietary choices or skipping meals.
2. Sedentary lifestyle or lack of physical activity.
3. Chronic stress.

Soul Cup Fillers:

1. Spending time in nature.
2. Engaging in creative activities.
3. Experiencing joy.

Soul Cup Drainers:

1. Lack of personal boundaries.
2. Disconnected from BE-ing and experiencing energy leaks.

3. Ignoring personal values or neglecting self-care routines.

After listing your cup fillers and drainers, take a moment to consider how you can bring more of the cup fillers into your daily routine. Aim to prioritise these activities and remain mindful of your drainers.

Feeling Energised

Britt was desperate for energy to return and to ease into her new wellbeing practices, but we took a gentle approach, gradually helping her detach from her constant busyness. We strategically focused on replenishing Britt's Wellbeing Cups with activities that ignited her excitement and fulfilled her needs. We discussed the significance of acceptance and patience and acknowledged that true transformation takes time and there are no instant solutions. By encouraging Britt to stay committed to her wellbeing practices, we instilled the understanding that consistency would lead to long-term sustainability. We ensured that all aspects of her wellbeing – body, mind and soul – received attention.

After a few months of adjusting to her new routine, her energy returned, enabling her to fully engage in and enjoy life. She felt like herself again and no longer felt like she was constantly juggling tasks and struggling to stay afloat; instead, she felt as though everything was flowing effortlessly. She felt grounded and balanced, and with her newfound energy, she made the decision to enrol in an online study program in animal care, a subject that had fascinated her since childhood. She also started a vegetable garden together with her children, dedicating hours every week to nurture her plants.

Through the practice of the Wellbeing Cups, Britt not only avoided the path to complete burnout but also discovered that her mind, body and soul connection can guide her towards sustainable long-term achievements.

Prioritising our wellbeing as a sustainable practice enables us to fill our cups and enjoy more energy and clarity of thought. This creates a finely tuned connection between our mind, body and soul, giving us invaluable wisdom that sustains balance in our lives. As we feel balanced and energised, we not only gain a clear perspective of our capabilities but also our potential and opportunities for personal growth.

Motivated to realise our full potential, we can shed any inclination to play small. Instead, we strive for achievements, recognising our inherent worth and embracing our authentic selves with gratitude, for what we as an individual bring to the table. This alignment with our true selves feels comforting – like returning home – offering a secure foundation from which to venture into more achievements. In this space of alignment, we can access an infinite well of inspiration, our own source of creativity and innovation that propels us forward for a life of fulfilment.

In the next chapter, we explore the Contribution Stage, where we explore why contributing gives us a sense of purpose and fulfilment, enriching our lives with deeper meaning and a sense of belonging.

Recall our exploration of the emotion Drained in Part 1, where we applied the SFUC method. Now, let's revisit this section armed with our understanding of the Achievement Stage.

SFUC Method for Drained:

Stop: Take a deep breath.

Feel: Take a moment to ask yourself, "How am I feeling?"

Example: I don't have the energy to participate. Everything seems too hard, and I don't know what to do. I have lost or am losing the ability to feel excited about my current life situation. I feel depleted and am in a state of imbalance, making me feel empty and exhausted.

Understand: Why am I feeling like this?

My mind, body and soul are yearning for a recharge, but I have nothing left to give. As my reserves are getting lower, I feel the need to replenish. An ongoing and accumulating stressor slowly is or was sapping away my energy reserves. It's like a constant drain on my mental and emotional resources.

Connect: Try answering the following questions:

1. What creates energy for me, and what takes it away?
2. In which areas of my life am I neglecting myself?
3. In what areas of my life am I not fully embracing my potential?
4. What activities or experiences bring me a sense of joy and fulfilment?
5. What are my true emotions and thoughts regarding this specific situation in my life that's causing me to feel drained?

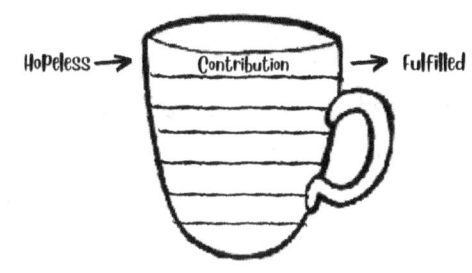

The Contribution Stage

The Contribution Stage is the final stage of our Wellbeing Cup. It's truly a magical stage, where we discover the joy of giving back from a place of abundance and authenticity. Here, our journey of personal growth continues to unfold, expanding our ability to make meaningful contributions to the world around us. In this stage, our focus shifts outwards, guided by the core principle that when we embrace our authentic selves, we become immensely valuable to society.

You may wonder what contribution actually means. Contribution refers to the act of giving, sharing or providing something valuable to others or to society as a whole. It involves using our talents, resources, time or efforts for the benefit of others, with the intention of making a positive impact or difference in their lives. Contribution can take many forms, including volunteering, donating, mentoring, teaching, creating art, innovating or simply offering support and kindness to those in need. It is a fundamental aspect of human interaction and societal progress, fostering collaboration, empathy, acceptance and interconnectedness. The magic of contribution is that it enriches both the giver and the recipient, creating a deep sense of fulfilment.

Social freedom and wellbeing are closely intertwined with contribution. Social freedom is all about being yourself and feeling good about it, while wellbeing is about living a fulfilling life. Together they create the foundation from which we are empowered to give back to others and society.

You might find it interesting to know that contributing to others is beneficial in many ways. Studies show that when we give to others, it activates reward pathways in the brain, resulting in feelings of joy and satisfaction. It can also help us create bonds with people who share similar interests and values, making us feel more connected. Plus, contributing gives us a sense of purpose and fulfilment, enriching our lives with deeper meaning and a sense of belonging. Furthermore, contribution presents opportunities for personal growth by encouraging us to venture beyond our comfort zones, reach our potential and use our unique talents.

Marian

Marian, a dedicated professional and mother of three, recently made the transition from a busy career to retirement. With her children now grown and living away, she found herself struggling with feelings of emptiness and hopelessness about her situation. Spending much of her time at home, she felt that she was at a loss, isolated and that she lacked the social interactions that once inspired her and filled her workdays. On top of that, Marian realised she had few relationships outside of her professional life, leaving her longing for a deeper sense of purpose and connection.

In our sessions, Marian expressed her longing for change but felt unsure how to initiate it. Recognising her need for fulfilment, I introduced Marian to the value of the concept of GCC (Growth, Community and Connection), in which we emphasise the importance of nurturing personal growth, giving back to the community and fostering meaningful connections with others. By incorporating these principles into her daily life, we aimed to develop a greater sense of fulfilment.

We explored various opportunities for Marian to engage with her community. Given her successful navigation of the Action and Achievement Stages during her career, Marian felt confident and ready to give back from a place of abundance and authenticity. Volunteer work at the local women's shelter emerged as Marian's choice for community engagement, providing her with a platform to channel her energy and talents, while creating meaningful connections with like-minded people.

Additionally, I encouraged Marian to explore further opportunities for self-growth, suggesting she explore new hobbies or studies aligned with her interests and values, especially now that she has more time available. By investing in her personal development, Marian would not only enrich her own life but also continue to fill her cup and increase her capacity to contribute meaningfully to others.

The Value Of GCC

The concept of GCC stands for Growth, Community and Connection. It focuses on three essential aspects of fulfilment:

1. Growth involves continuous learning and self-improvement, whether through acquiring new skills, pursuing education or personal development activities. Growth allows us to expand our capabilities, explore new opportunities and reach our full potential.
2. Community refers to the connections we have with others and the sense of belonging we derive from being part of a group.
3. Connection involves meaningful interactions with others, whether through empathy, acceptance, understanding or shared experiences. Creating deep connections enhances our sense of fulfilment and wellbeing.

If you find yourself struggling with feelings of hopelessness or loneliness, incorporating the GCC concept can be transformative. This approach helps you to create positive change in your life, reinforcing your authentic value and giving a sense of optimism for the future.

Navigating Emotions through Contribution

The Contribution Stage offers a space to navigate feelings of hopelessness. Helping others or making a positive impact can help alleviate these emotions. Contributing to something meaningful can remind us that we have the ability to make a difference in the world, reinstating a sense of purpose and direction. By connecting with others, seeking community support and engaging in acts of contribution, we not only manage these emotions but also reconnect with ourselves. In essence, by reaching outwards, we find our way back inwards, rediscovering our sense of self and meaning.

Identifying feelings of hopelessness can be challenging, as it can present as a vague sense of unease or dissatisfaction. Signs may include statements like, 'What is the point', 'I can't see a way out' or 'This will never improve'. This may be accompanied by feelings of loneliness and a lack of inspiration. Questions about the purpose and meaning of life may also arise, prompting us to ponder our existence and the value of our contributions.

Feeling hopeless, at its core, is the absence of hope or optimism and a belief that positive change is beyond reach. It can show up as a suffocating sense of defeat. It can leave us feeling powerless, trapped and resigned to our circumstances.

In moments of hopelessness, it can be beneficial to shift our focus outwards rather than inwards for solutions. Asking ourselves questions such as:

- What support systems are available to me?
- How can I connect with my community?
- What opportunities exist for meaningful connections?
- Where can I find avenues for personal growth and self-development?

These inquiries can help point us towards resources and strategies that make us feel supported and provide a sense of purpose. It is also important to recognise that we can't do everything alone and that we're not meant to – reaching out to others for help and guidance can provide valuable support during difficult times.

Whether we're caring for an elderly parent, supporting a loved one with a disability, working as a mentor or volunteering in our community, engaging in any form of contribution demands a considerable amount of energy. While these acts can be deeply fulfilling, it's important to stay conscious of safeguarding our energy and ensure that our Wellbeing Cups remain topped up, so we can give from a place of abundance, particularly during the Contribution Stage, where our attention is directed towards giving and supporting others, and it can be easy to overlook our own needs.

Theo

Theo, an artist, finds himself at a crossroad in his creative journey. While deeply passionate about his art, he feels a longing for more meaning and connection in his life. Creating art has been a solitary process for Theo, and while he values this experience, he yearns to connect with like-minded people and contribute to something greater than himself.

In our sessions, Theo expresses his desire to find his tribe, a community where he can be himself and feel accepted. He also wants to focus on contribution, feeling a strong pull to share his art with the world and uplift others. However, every time he takes steps towards this goal, he feels overwhelmed with feelings of inadequacy and negative self-talk. Theo worries about how his work will be received, questioning his worthiness and fearing criticism from others.

Together, we explore the importance of intentional action and staying focused on the bigger picture. We delve into Theo's values, which include being of service, living with integrity and using his art to inspire others. By shifting his focus away from self-doubt and towards his desire to uplift and inspire, focusing outwards instead of inwards, Theo begins to gain clarity on his direction.

To address his feelings of vulnerability and self-doubt, we incorporate the Growth Edge Exercise into our sessions. This helps him commit to stepping outside his comfort zone and embracing his full potential rather than hiding behind lim-

iting beliefs. We also incorporate mindfulness techniques to help Theo stay present at the moment and quiet his mind from worries about the future.

The Growth Edge Exercise

When we commit to contribution, we showcase our individuality by bringing forth our unique talents, strengths and values. This blend, combined with our aspirations, passion and dedication, empowers us to make a real, positive impact on the world around us and brings us closer to realising our dreams.

However, this often pushes us beyond our comfort zones, stirring up feelings of uncertainty and fear. To remain true to being our beautiful selves and stay driven by purpose, we can turn to the Growth Edge Exercise. This tool helps us stretch beyond our comfort zones, even when faced with fear, limiting beliefs and negative self-talk. These challenges arise precisely because we are pushing the boundaries of what is familiar to us.

Feeling vulnerable and uncertain is a natural response when we venture into new territory. However, by recognising that growth often lies beyond this discomfort, we can shift our focus to the bigger picture. This shift allows us to navigate challenges while staying committed to the growth process.

Here are some steps to guide you through the Growth Edge Exercise:

1. Begin by reflecting on your dreams and aspirations, as they often highlight areas where growth is needed. Where can you take steps to bring these into reality?

2. Pay real attention to your feelings when considering stepping outside your comfort zone. Do you notice any discomfort, fear or resistance? Do any negative self-talk or limiting beliefs arise?
3. Take some time to explore these thoughts and feelings to gain insight into how they might be hindering your progress. The Inner Voice Exercise introduced in the Awareness Stage can be a valuable tool to help reframe these thoughts. Begin by acknowledging and writing down any negative self-talk or limiting beliefs that surface. Then, challenge these thoughts by asking yourself questions such as: Is this belief based on facts or assumptions? What evidence supports or contradicts this belief? How might I reframe this thought in a more empowering or constructive way?
4. Acknowledge that experiencing feeling vulnerable when stepping outside your comfort zone is a natural part of the growth process. Instead of resisting or avoiding these feelings, accept them as signals of your willingness to stretch and evolve.
5. Believe in yourself and your ability to effect change, understanding that staying true to yourself is key to growth and that your unique perspective is valuable.
6. Take deliberate action aligned with your values and integrity, that way you know you are contributing meaningfully to your personal growth.
7. If you feel overwhelmed, remember you can take small steps.

8. Connect with your inner wisdom to guide your decisions and actions. Keep your Mind, Body and Soul cups topped up so you can rely on your inner voice to provide clarity and direction, especially during moments of uncertainty or indecision.
9. Shift your focus outwards, considering the broader impact of your contributions to others and the world around you. By expanding your perspective beyond yourself, you gain insight into how your actions ripple outwards.
10. Challenge yourself to step outside your comfort zone, even if it's just with small steps, and then take time to reflect on the insights gained from these experiences. Use these insights to inform your future actions and continue pushing the boundaries of your comfort zone, knowing that each step forward brings you closer.
11. Celebrate your successes, no matter how small they may seem, and allow them to fuel your continued growth.

By following these steps, you can gain clarity on your growth edge and take meaningful action to reach your full potential.

Theo began stepping off his comfort zone by participating in local small art exhibitions, where he had the opportunity to meet other artists. Much to his surprise, as he shared his art, he found that people not only resonated deeply with his artwork but also expressed a genuine interest in learning more about him. They drew inspiration and a sense of connection from the vulnerability he expressed through his art; feeling that it permitted them to be vulnerable as well, they felt seen and understood.

As a result, Theo also began to feel seen and accepted for who he truly was. Inspired by the positive reception of his art, he became more willing to show up as himself. Recognising that he had previously struggled with being fully seen and had been hiding behind his art, he realised that it was time to step into his full potential.

By engaging in contribution, both the giver and receiver gained. If Theo had allowed his limiting beliefs and fears to stop him, none of this would have transpired.

Theo's next step was a brave one – a joint exhibition with several artists he admired, aimed at raising funds for a charity. This opportunity was exciting for him. Collaborating with other artists and working on a larger scale meant pushing even further out of his comfort zone, but he was determined to take on the challenge.

Despite his initial excitement, Theo soon grew frustrated with himself. He felt pressured to surpass his previous artistic achievements, and this weighed heavily on him, made worse by his comparisons to his fellow artists. Overwhelmed by feelings of inadequacy, he began to doubt his own abilities. Doubts about the upcoming exhibition crept in, leaving him feeling hopeless and unsure of how to proceed.

In a moment of desperation, he told his fellow artists about his struggles. He opened up about his fear that his work wouldn't measure up to theirs, expecting judgement or criticism in return. However, to his surprise, many of them shared similar doubts and insecurities. Instead of judgement, they offered support and encouragement, expressing admiration for his work and gratitude for his participation in the exhibition.

This sense of understanding among his fellow artists gave Theo renewed determination. He threw himself into his work, painting tirelessly day after day. He curated an impressive collection of works that were raw, vulnerable and deeply reflective of his inner self. The exhibition, as a result, was a success. Theo and the other artists felt connected to the community and proud of the impact they had made. This boosted Theo's confidence and inspired him to dream even bigger for his next exhibition.

When we are unapologetically ourselves, we can genuinely connect with others. This is an expression of social freedom. The Contribution Stage and social freedom go hand in hand, creating an environment of understanding, empathy and support. Real self-acceptance, both for ourselves and others, lays the foundation for establishing a space where belonging and authenticity flourish. This acceptance in social interactions becomes the cornerstone for people to feel valued, fostering positive connections and relationships. It sets the stage for a supportive community where everyone can freely express themselves without the fear of judgement. By fostering this kind of culture of inclusivity and understanding, we also fuel personal growth and healing.

Contribution and Its Ripple Effect

The act of contribution goes beyond simply giving back or making a positive impact on others; it's also about creating a space where we can fully express ourselves. When we contribute from a place of authenticity and integrity, we not only uplift others but also nurture our own wellbeing.

By embracing our unique talents, values and passions, we create opportunities to connect with like-minded people and build meaningful relationships. This sense of belonging and acceptance leads us to express our creativity, share our gifts with the world and pursue our dreams without hesitation.

Engaging in a life of contribution allows us to align our actions with our values and create positive change and a ripple effect in our surroundings. Whether through volunteering, mentoring or expressing ourselves through art, all forms of contribution reflect our commitment to making a difference and leaving behind a legacy.

In essence, contribution serves as a cornerstone of wellbeing and social freedom, empowering us to be ourselves, connect with others and lead a purpose-driven life. By embracing these principles and actively making meaningful contributions, we can experience a sense of fulfilment and joy that extends far beyond individual achievements.

Your Wellbeing Toolbox

Throughout this book, we've travelled together on a journey towards wellbeing and a deeper connection with our inner selves. This path has led us towards significant positive changes and ultimately feeling fulfilled as the best version of ourselves. Through regular engagement in wellbeing practices, we've experienced that this state of fulfilment is within reach for all of us.

As illustrated below, our path through the various stages within the Wellbeing Cup has shown us the process of both 'letting go' and 'receiving' at the same time, as we learnt to release what no longer serves us and welcomed new experiences and insights into our lives, gradually guiding us towards fulfilment. Simultaneously, our exploration of social freedom has provided us with insights and strategies for balancing our emotions. By merging these elements, we've created a pathway to connect with our authentic selves, attain mental clarity and nurture our overall wellbeing.

Having explored the seven stages of the Wellbeing Cup together, we've covered significant ground. Throughout the chapters, along the way, we've assembled a toolbox filled with wellbeing tools and practices, ready to support us in our daily lives and when confronting challenges.

With our toolbox fully stocked, we are empowered and prepared to take on whatever may arise. As we approach the conclusion of our path to wellbeing, it is now time to begin our journey back home.

Recall our exploration of the emotion of Hopelessness in Part 1, where we applied the SFUC method. Now, let's revisit this section armed with our understanding of the Contribution Stage.

SFUC Method for Hopeless:

Stop: Take a deep breath.

Feel: Take a moment to ask yourself, "How am I feeling?"

Example: I feel like there is no light at the end of the tunnel; I don't know what to do.

Understand: Why am I feeling like this?

I feel like this because I feel trapped in this situation. I can neither see a way out nor how it can improve, therefore I feel like giving up.

Connect: Try answering the following questions:

1. Where can I take steps to make progress and improve my situation?
2. What does it require for me to feel supported?
3. Where do I have meaningful connections with others, and where can I find my supportive community?
4. How can I keep developing those connections further with my community?
5. Is it possible to create a plan, to take the steps required to create those connections?
6. What areas in my life represent opportunities for growth?

Part 3
The Journey Back Home

The Journey Back Home

Before we dive into the core of Part 3, I encourage you to pause and visit the artwork on the previous page. How does it resonate with you? Personally, I'm deeply touched by it, as it symbolises for me the power of nature to uplift, inspire and connect us to something greater than ourselves. For me, it evokes feelings of vastness and boundlessness, yet it also offers a sense of comfort and promise.

I often encourage my clients to spend time surrounded by nature. Because something transformative happens when they do; it's like they receive a gentle reminder of their freedom to be their authentic selves.

I think this happens because nature, with its beauty and imperfections, serves as a reflection of our innermost selves. It is the purest form of BE-ing and demonstrates the importance of uniqueness. For example, no two trees are exactly alike, yet each one is equally important and deserving of admiration. Similarly, the way flowers bloom in all their glory, in their varied forms and colours, creates a captivating vision reminding us of the importance of diversity.

As you may have gathered, I'm a passionate advocate for the healing power of nature and its capacity to evoke a deep sense of connection to our authentic selves. Whether we seek a brief moment of reflection or are on a longer healing journey, nature stands ready to support us. If you're feeling the need for this kind of embrace, consider immersing yourself in nature daily.

What's Next

Life is filled with ups and downs, challenges and triumphs. Regardless of where we are on our individual paths, we all encounter struggles at various points in our lives. It's the nature of existence, and it's something that will likely continue to be so. What sets us apart, though, is how we respond to these challenges. Do we feel equipped and empowered to make the necessary changes to turn things around?

Throughout this book, we've explored a variety of tools and practices designed to guide you through challenging times and inspire personal growth. From understanding and regulating emotions though to the seven stages of wellbeing, each chapter has been a stepping stone to support you on your path.

Now, as you continue your journey, I imagine you actively apply these tools and practices, creating the foundation for your dream life. Or maybe you like to ponder on what you've read so far for a bit before making any changes in your life. Either way, I also understand that life can get busy, and it's easy to forget or feel overwhelmed by the sheer amount of information presented in this book.

Therefore, I've created a mind map for future reference. This visual tool serves as a quick reference guide, allowing you to easily locate specific tools or revisit emotions as needed. This resource provides a comprehensive overview of the key concepts covered in this book and as a reminder that you have the knowledge, strength and tools necessary to overcome any obstacles that come your way.

As we've explored throughout this book, true freedom is found in our ability to understand and regulate our emotions. While we can't control external factors like how society treats us, or the triggers in our daily lives, we can control how we respond to our emotions. With this understanding, we have the power to shape our own lives and pursue the direction we desire. It won't always be easy; in fact, it may require hard work at times, but with the right tools, a deep understanding of our wellbeing and a strong belief in ourselves, we are fully capable of achieving this.

We possess everything necessary to embrace life wholeheartedly, without waiting for external validation or circumstances to guide us. Each of us has the inherent right to social freedom and wellbeing. When we seize the moment and live life to the fullest, embrace our uniqueness and share our dreams and love with the world, we are not only fulfilling our own purpose but also contributing to making the world a better place.

The journey back home is a return to our true selves. Despite the trials and lessons we endure, we can always find our way back. No matter how far we've strayed, it patiently awaits our return. As we gather wisdom on our path, we realise that home has been with us all along, accompanying us on our journey.

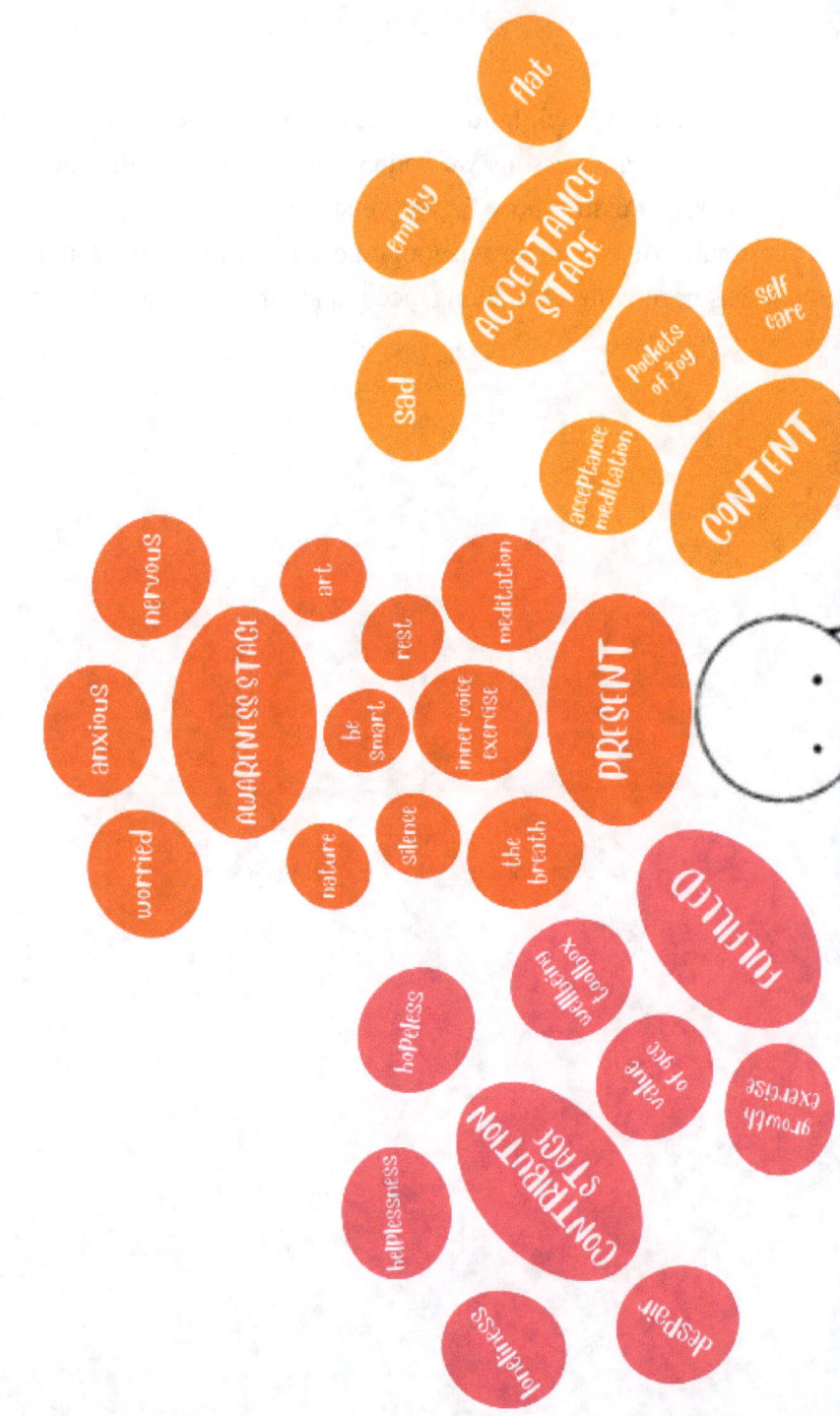

Home Is Where the Heart Is

If there's one crucial takeaway I hope you gain from this book, it's this: You are perfect just the way you are. This fundamental truth is a cornerstone of true freedom and inner peace. When you fully accept yourself, you unlock the door to living with an open heart, allowing for immense growth and a deep connection with the inner strength that resides in all of us.

This inner strength becomes the driving force behind showing up for ourselves and others every day. Moreover, as we share our love and authenticity with the world, we discover that it is returned to us tenfold. The more we give of ourselves, the more abundance we receive in return. This beautiful exchange reinforces the truth that we are inherently perfect and worthy of love and acceptance just as we are.

So, if ever you find yourself feeling lost or uncertain, remember to trust in the wisdom of your heart. Your heart is your compass, guiding you back to your true essence and reminding you that home is not a place but a state of being. Home is where the heart resides, and you, my dear reader, are already there.

Thank you for travelling on this journey with me.

I wish you a life of fulfilment and an abundance of love.

—Deborah

A Picture Speaks a Thousand Words

In this book, I wanted to create an inclusive experience that transcended barriers of written communication. To achieve this, I sought to incorporate engaging visual elements alongside the written content. Fortunately, I had the privilege of collaborating with the talented artist, Jett Fahey, whose intuitive understanding of my vision brought it to life in ways I could have never imagined.

Jett is not just an artist; he is a multidisciplinary creative powerhouse. His diverse talents span from digital drawings to large-scale paintings to intricate sculptures. Jett lives in a world of eccentricity and art with his family and two cats, and his artworks exude a mystical quality that resonates deeply with viewers. Each piece seems to transcend reality, evoking emotions and feelings that words alone struggle to convey.

Working with Jett was an absolute delight. He effortlessly transformed my messy sketches and abstract ideas into stunning visual masterpieces. It was as if he could read my mind, understanding the essence of each chapter and translating it into captivating imagery. Seeing how his interpretations brought the book to life nearly brought me to tears, as his artwork beautifully captured the essence of social freedom.

I am deeply grateful to Jett for his professionalism, dedication and incredible talent. His contributions have enriched this book beyond measure. Thank you, Jett, for sharing your gift with the world and helping to bring my vision to life in an impactful way. Your pictures speak a thousand words.

Seeking Help

Together, we've explored various tools and insights to support you on your path. However, it's important to recognise that sometimes, these tools may not be enough on their own. That's where seeking help from compassionate professionals comes into play.

First and foremost, it's essential to understand that seeking help is not a sign of weakness. On the contrary, it's a brave acknowledgement of your own struggles and a willingness to take steps towards healing and growth. Just like the clients you've encountered within these pages, they have taken courageous steps forward, and their progress is a testament to the power of seeking support.

When dealing with mental health challenges, it's important to be kind to yourself and acknowledge that you're not alone. There are numerous forms of support available, including therapists, coaches and counsellors, who are dedicated to assisting you on your journey. These professionals offer a safe and non-judgemental space where you can explore your emotions, gain insights and develop coping strategies.

It's also important to recognise that we're all at different stages of our journey, and there's no one-size-fits-all approach to seeking help. When considering the right support for you, it's essential to take into account your individual needs and circumstances.

For example, if you are navigating grief in the Acceptance Stage, a grief counsellor or therapist may provide valuable support and guidance. If you are working through the Action Stage and ready to take the next step, a specialised coach could help you develop practical strategies to move forward. And if you're seeking to contribute and grow further in the Contribution Stage, a mentor who has walked a similar path may offer invaluable insights and encouragement. Ultimately, remember that you deserve support tailored to your unique needs.

As we come to the end of this book, please know that our journey together doesn't have to end here. If you feel inspired to explore any of the practices further or if you're seeking personalised guidance and support, I invite you to reach out. Your wellbeing is important to me, and I am committed to supporting you on your journey towards a more fulfilling and meaningful life. Please feel free to contact me at deborahdevaal@gmail.com. Together, we can continue to explore, learn and grow.

Acknowledgements

Words cannot adequately express the immense gratitude I feel towards everyone who has supported me in the creation of this book.

First and foremost, I'd like to say a massive thank you to Lesley Roulston. Lesley, your exceptional understanding of the English language, coupled with your patience and encouragement, has been invaluable. I have learnt so much from you, and I am extremely grateful for the countless hours you dedicated to proofreading and providing meticulous feedback. You are truly a legend.

To my parents, Annemarie and Niek, despite us being miles apart, you are my biggest cheerleaders, and your unwavering support has kept me going through all the wonderful highs and lows that come with writing a book. Our weekly conversations, filled with love and wisdom, kept me grounded and reminded me of my inner strength. Thank you for believing in me and encouraging me to pursue my dreams.

Special gratitude goes to Jett Fahey, whose intuitive understanding of my vision breathed life into this book through his captivating imagery. Your talent and dedication have added depth and beauty to these pages, and I am immensely grateful for your contributions.

A heartfelt thank-you to all my loved ones, friends and family for their patience and understanding as I dedicated myself to writing this book, often disappearing into my own world for days at a time.

Last but certainly not least, I extend my sincerest thanks to you, dear reader, for picking up a copy of this book and journeying alongside me. Your curiosity and open-mindedness inspire me, and I hope our paths cross again in the future.

With heartfelt gratitude,

—Deborah Devaal

About the Author

Deborah Devaal is a dedicated Art Therapist and Wellbeing Coach who lives on the East Coast of Australia and is known for her integrated approach to holistic wellbeing. Her diverse array of practices aims to nurture individuals' emotional and mental health, fostering resilience and promoting personal growth. With a primary focus on mental health, Deborah specialises in understanding and navigating the complexities of emotional challenges.

Drawing from therapeutic examples, practical techniques and supportive strategies, Deborah empowers people to confront life's obstacles and enhance their coping mechanisms. Whether through personalised therapy sessions, online programs or community engagements, Deborah's goal is to alleviate suffering and facilitate personal growth and fulfilment.

In her first book, Social Freedom: The Path to Wellbeing, Deborah guides readers through challenges with understanding and hope. Her approach emphasises empathy, compassion and empowerment, providing a roadmap for navigating life's ups and downs with resilience and strength. Through her insightful perspectives and practical strategies, Deborah offers readers a transformative journey towards greater emotional and mental wellbeing, empowering them to overcome obstacles and thrive in all aspects of their lives.

www.ingramcontent.com/pod-product-compliance
Lightning Source LLC
Chambersburg PA
CBHW051430290426
44109CB00016B/1502